A FERRET IN THE VESTRY

3

013

10

'2

A FERRET IN THE VESTRY

Carol Hathorne

CHIVERS LARGE PRINT
BATH

British Library Cataloguing in Publication Data available

This Large Print edition published by Chivers Press, Bath, 2002.
Published by arrangement with the author.

U.K. Hardcover ISBN 0 7540 4819 5
U.K. Softcover ISBN 0 7540 4820 9

Copyright © Carol Hathorne 1995

The right of Carol Hathorne to be identified as the author of this work
has been asserted by her in accordance with the Copyright, Designs and
Patents Act, 1988.

Disclaimer
You will not find Netherley Bank on any map of the Black Country.
Similarly, the characters portrayed in *A Ferret in the Vestry* are fictional—
ie composite archetypes. None is intended to represent any actual one
person, living or dead, who I have encountered in my own ministry.
(This, naturally, does not apply to my own family, members of which are
referred to by their real names.)

Printed and bound in Great Britain by
BOOKCRAFT, Midsomer Norton, Somerset

To the members of General Synod who said
'YES!'

PREFACE

by the Bishop of Worcester

So great a step as ordaining women to the priesthood was bound to provoke authors at every level of writing. Some have produced theological works but few have produced popular writing such as this.

This easily read book is to be commended. It is in the style of a popular novel and gives insight into the multifarious activities of a parish priest in the Church of England. Inevitably it is very funny in places. It has been said that although there are drawbacks to membership of an ancient institution like the Church of England, there are also vast opportunities for laughter and fun. I will say no more. You must read on and I dare to think your understanding of the life of an ordained person will be enlarged.

Philip Worcester

FOREWORD

What comes through Carol Hathorne's book is great warmth and understanding.

She has a God-given gift of empathy, coupled with common sense, humour, and above all spiritual perception. In these pages I met a priest, one who is able to exercise her priestly ministry without losing sight of her own humanity, and femininity. Here is someone who knows what life is all about—she knows all about the problems of today, she is right there in it, she's come up the hard way. The 'Black Country' is a tough environment, and the folk who live there are quick to recognise anything and anyone who is not genuine. You can't pull the wool over their eyes. But with someone like Carol they will share themselves, be encouraged to reach out to God and others, and catch the vision knowing they have a friend, a companion to help them on the way.

Her book captures and enlightens in a delightful way, revealing not only the joys and sorrows of a woman priest, but also of a truly shared ministry, husband and wife, Anglican and Methodist, and those delightful and sometimes infuriating people who make up Netherley Bank. An 'inside story' with a difference!

I gladly and wholeheartedly commend this book. This is *not* 'The Vicar of Dibley', it's the real thing!

The Rev. Margaret Cundiff,
Broadcasting Officer,
Diocese of York

CHAPTER ONE

'It *bit* me!' The young woman, coming through the vestry door with her fiancé, let out an enormous scream.

'W-what?' Standing there in my cassock, ready to welcome the St Benedict's marriage preparation class, I stared from her to the flagged stone floor. Just in time to see a small, furry rodent shoot between us.

'A rat!' I immediately thought, and shuddered. But the young man, holding his fiancée's finger aloft—a finger showing tiny pin-pricks of blood—said: 'It's a ferret! I thought something was following us across the graveyard!'

'Close the door, Reverend,' he instructed me urgently, 'before it gets into the church!'

Already seated in the grand, pillared nave of St Benedict's parish church, Netherley Bank's 'cathedral of the Black Country', were a dozen couples, waiting, with varying degrees of interest and impatience, for the preparation session to begin. They were all due to be married that summer and autumn, and for many of them, this was their first time in church.

Their heads shot up as if by a signal as I catapulted backwards through the inner door and slammed it firmly shut.

1

'You'll have to excuse me,' I told my waiting congregation, 'but we've got a ferret in the vestry!'

There was a moment's stunned, disbelieving silence, as if they all wondered if this might be a new evangelism ploy. Then, as I realised the incongruity of the situation, I laughed, and so did they.

'It's perfectly true,' I began to explain, as I went towards the lectern. 'It followed a young couple across the graveyard, and now it's bitten . . .'

'Honestly! What a performance!' The heads all turned as from behind the edifice of St Benedict's great church organ, there emerged the bearded face and bald head of Clarke Pettisgrew, our ex-cathedral choir master and director of music.

A plump, bristling little man who made no secret of the fact that he thought the Church of England had gone insane the day it decided to ordain women, he never passed up an opportunity to try and redress the balance.

Putting down the music he had been sorting, he marched past me, saying down his nose, 'I'll go and get rid of it, if you really can't bring yourself to!'

Unable to contain my curiosity, I followed him at a safe distance back into the vestry. I was just in time to see him stoop, then jump balletically about three feet into the air, his right forefinger extended painfully in front of him: 'Oooer! You little . . . !'

The ferret, undeterred, darted under the nearest bench.

'What do we do now?' asked the young man who had brought the creature in while Clarke jumped around clutching his injury and talking about tetanus jabs. 'I don't know the first thing about ferrets!'

'Neither do I,' I confessed, 'but I think I know a man who does. Just wait here while I nip to the vicarage and use the phone.'

My colleague, Revd Geoff Hanson, who lived at St Benedict's vicarage next door was out at a school governor's meeting, but his wife, Jane, let me in. After listening open mouthed to my rather garbled account of the night's events, she agreed we should definitely send for the verger.

Tom Jenkins had been verger at St Benedict's for over forty years. A somewhat wizened octogenarian, he knew everything and everybody in Netherley Bank, and was a self-confessed jack of all trades.

He turned up on his rusty bike just as I finished the marriage preparation class and was seeing all the couples but one off the premises, the ferret couple having gone with Clarke to the local Russets Road hospital.

' 'E's bin attracted by the light, see, vicar,' he said knowingly as, pulling a little, he got on his hands and knees in front of the bench. 'Probl'y bin left down sum rabbit 'ole over the bonk.'

I stared in surprise at the tortoise-like face close to mine. 'You mean people still use them for catching rabbits?' I asked.

In spite of the returned greenery that came as a result of losing its industry, to waves of recession, Netherley Bank couldn't, by any stretch of the imagination, be called rural.

'Oh, ar,' Tom assured me with a grunt. 'Plenty o' good rabbitin' an rattin' round 'ere, vicar! Allus 'as bin!'

Bending further, he thrust his gloved hand under the bench. 'Come on, beaut. I wo' 'urt yer!

''E'll come wi' me now,' he whispered, putting his face close to mine again a few moments later. 'Just goo out an' switch the light off, will yer, vicar, an' leave room fer me to run out wi' me torch?'

I nodded gravely, scrambled to my feet in the hampering cassock and tiptoed to the door.

In no time at all, Tom was to be seen, running briskly across the moonlit graveyard, the torchlight spilling out a path in front of him and the ferret running, dog like, after.

'We'll, I've heard of fishers of men!' Geoff remarked, getting out of his car outside the vicarage just in time to witness the amazing scene. 'I hope this isn't going to be a new trend!'

That night, I lay curled up in bed with Mark, my Methodist minister husband whom I had married the summer before. The house was quiet, his children, my two stepsons, fast asleep.

I thought back to the events, not only of that day, but of the whole amazing chapter of incidents that had brought me here. To be Netherley Bank's first woman curate. And one of the first women priests to be ordained in the Church of England.

Born and bred in the Black Country, in the days when factory hooters and industrial smog were part of the everyday landscape of life, I had no Christian background until, at the age of ten, I was told by my cousin Eva that there was a Sunday School in Great Bridgley where they gave you sweets.

In the 1950s when, in our house at any rate, sweets only came once a week with a kindly, visiting aunt, this was too good a chance to miss. So my brother and I went along, with Eva, to a little tin hut, a disused air raid shelter, down by the railway line and the town slaughter house.

There, though first seduced by a multi-coloured gob-stopper, I soon discovered other joys. Star cards, stamped each week you attended, mistily colourful stickers with verses from the Bible, and the promise, like Christmas, of a book prize, and an outing to some big park in the summer.

But, though I would have denied it later, I discovered much more than that. For one

Sunday night in that tin hut, heated by a pot bellied stove with a pipe going through the roof, I listened with all my being to the words of the pastor, Oliver Paskin.

A tall man with a bush of dark hair that spread to his startling eyebrows, Oliver seemed to me in those days to be a giant, not only in stature, but in the sheer power of his message and ministry.

In a world of confusion and uncertainty, he knew and lived the life-changing truth of the gospel. The night he urged us to make that commitment—to open our hearts there and then to the Lord Jesus—he might have been speaking to me alone.

Many years of doubt and searching followed that initial stirring. But it was what had led, undoubtedly, to my eventual training on the West Midlands Ministerial Training course at Queen's college, Birmingham. There, American born Mark had been a tutor and, both smarting from painful, failed first marriages, we had met, and fallen in love.

Now, with a wonder and joy that the majority of our congregations seemed to share, we combined our vocations in a 'truly ecumenical, though sometimes slightly crazy household, and many shared Anglican /Methodist services, here in the Black Country.

'You awake, darling?' I started as Mark spoke gently, near my ear.

'Mmmm,' I yawned and stretched and

moved closer into the warm circle of his arms. 'I've been thinking about Oliver,' I said, sleepily. 'You know, the gob-stopper man? I s'pose Tom Jenkins reminds me of him, a bit.'

I broke off, remembering the laughter at St Benedict's tonight, easing the initial awkwardness of the marriage couples, the way the offbeat situation had surprised and warmed them, making church a less alien, more welcoming place to be.

'Isn't it funny, when something's really quirky—that's when you know God's really there?'

'Mmmm,' Now it was Mark's turn to yawn and stretch. Glancing at the clock, I realised it was way past time to start sleeping and stop talking. I didn't need anybody to tell me that in my case, that gob-stopper had never worked!

CHAPTER TWO

Netherley Bank High Street was one long stream of traffic. At eight forty-five in the morning it was crazy even trying to cross it, but I had to because St Benedict's was on the other side. Huge and imposing, the parish church stood in splendid Gothic isolation at the foot of Barlow Hill, its rather cumbersome square tower belying the elegance of its interior.

Its patrons once the family of the earl of Dudley, St Benedict's had a high wide nave, just made for processions, held up by magnificent pillars of warm sandstone.

Although its grandeur was somewhat faded now, an air of mystery and majesty prevailed. So that I could well understand when one elderly parishioner with a long memory once told me:

'At St Benedict's, when I was a girl, you *tiptoed*!'

Taking a deep breath, I plunged rather than tiptoed across the traffic laden road. I grinned as I caught sight of one or two startled looks from drivers. People were still surprised to see a woman in a cassock, especially in a traditionally Anglo-Catholic working class area like this.

Once the road had been negotiated, the

walk up to the church was quite pleasant, skirting the old coppice commonland, where poachers once roamed, and local horse traders and rag and bone men still took advantage of free grazing for their animals.

Further on, past the children's playground, there was an area of reclaimed industrial wasteland that was fast turning into a haven for weekend ramblers.

The railway line which once took workers from Netherley Bank and coal from the earl's nearby mine right into the heart of a great and greedy steelworks had been uprooted now, leaving a deserted bridle path peopled by ghosts. On the steel works site itself, the huge, American style carbuncle of the Merrily Mall shopping centre flourished, drawing tourists from all over the country.

'Good morning.' Geoff was in the lady chapel, waiting quietly for me to join him for Morning Prayer.

A tall, good-natured man in his mid-forties, he had been at Netherley Bank for seven years. With his plain, rather serious face topped by a thatch of grey streaked, rusty hair, he had an air of quiet unflappability and good humour which was consoling to colleagues and parishioners alike.

I sat opposite him, grateful for the silence of St Benedict's after the mayhem of the road outside. It was like dipping luxuriously into a lovely, deep pool of cool serenity.

My thoughts drifted almost automatically back to the wonderful day in May when, after my ordination to the priesthood in Worcester cathedral, I had at last been able to celebrate Holy Communion behind St Benedict's great stone altar.

After we had finished our prayers, Geoff put down his books very slowly. I had worked with him long enough, as deacon and priest, to know there was something on his mind. As we began to walk along the south aisle of the church towards the door, he suddenly said:

'There are a few members of the congregation who, typically, have left it until now to register their disapproval of women priests, Carol.'

'Oh?' I stared at him in surprise, thinking again of that first mass. The pews were full to overflowing, not only with St Benedict's people, but the local Methodists from Mark's church. Some of my oldest friends, those who had witnessed my struggle to be ordained priest, had been in tears when they came up to receive Communion.

'Yes.' Geoff sighed as he opened the vestry door and led the way automatically towards the vicarage. 'You must have noticed a few gaps on a weekly basis, since you've been able to preside?'

I frowned. 'Well, the Fishers always warned me they'd go elsewhere,' I said, thinking of our one overtly 'born again' family, 'but if

10

anything, I think the pews have been fuller.'

Geoff unlocked the vicarage door and I followed him into the kitchen. 'Curiosity, I think, Carol,' he said regretfully, as he put the kettle on. 'It's still pretty new, don't forget, especially in this area. The thing that worries me is we'll get two separate congregations— one when you're on duty and the other for me!'

I sighed as I considered this possibility. 'Well, as Clarke would say, they do have the right to choose!'

Geoff's shoulders seemed very set as he turned to make the coffee. 'Ah, Clarke!' he said, not quite meeting my eye as we went into the study. 'The maestro's another matter altogether. He'll do as he's told while I'm around, but as you've already gathered, he's certainly not happy!'

That 'while I'm around' rang a warning bell I didn't want to hear. I thought instead of the times even before I was priested, when Clarke had simply refused to play certain hymns at our monthly Junior Church because they were too lively.

'Vicars in knickers, he calls you!' Geoff reminded me, with a sudden grin. 'It'd be quite clever, if it was original.'

'The thing that worries me is his attitude to church growth,' I confessed. 'Last time I complimented him on an anthem and said it was a pity there were only four people at

11

evensong to hear it, he told me very snootily that I didn't understand. We weren't in church for the congregation. It was purely for the glory of God!'

Clarke had also, on other occasions, made it more than obvious that he despised what he called 'common' clergy—those who spoke the same local accent as their congregations, and hadn't been educated at Oxbridge.

'I've told him it's about time the Church of England stopped sending muesli-eating vicars to chip-eating congregations,' I elaborated, 'but I don't think he agrees!'

'Yes, he's definitely one to watch on several counts,' Geoff said, before we took out our diaries. 'And no doubt there'll be others emerging from the woodwork now you're officially a priest. Just keep your head down, Reverend!'

That morning, I was due to go into Russets Road hospital to make some calls, and to take communion to Gladys Eliot, one of the stalwarts of our congregation who had broken her hip.

Gladys was a spritely seventy-year-old who had, for many years before her retirement, been landlady of one of the local pubs. Like many Black Country people, she believed in speaking her mind on all subjects, and on all occasions.

As I approached with my communion set, greeting others on the ward on my way, she

12

called lustily: 'I thought *yo'd* forgot me!'

'Now, Gladys, how could I do that?' I asked, rhetorically, as I sat in the padded vinyl chair beside her bed. 'How're you doing, anyway? And how's George?'

Gladys gave an expressive snort at the mention of her miniature dachshund, George Eliot. As always, I suppressed the desire to ask facetiously if he'd written any good books lately.

'Dow talk to me about 'im—'es in my bad books!' she said, thumping her pillows into submission before she lay back on them.

'Why?' I had been preparing to set up the communion on the locker top, but something in the ferocity of Gladys' tone made me stop. 'What's he been up to now?'

Gladys' generous mouth was pursed in disapproval but that did nothing to soften the decibels as she boomed, 'On'y 'avin' sex wi' the cushion, 'e was, while I lay waitin' fer the ambulance to come!'

'Oh.' There didn't seem anything else to say, and besides, I wouldn't have been able to get a word in edgewise.

'Ar,' Gladys went on expressively, 'I o'ny 'ope 'e aye at it at our Mabel's while I'm in 'ere. 'Er bloke's one o' them Joviah witnesses—Cor stand 'em meself!'

Hoping there weren't any JW's in the ward, I suggested we draw the curtains round the bed while I gave Gladys her communion.

For a while, she was quiet and reflective, and I remembered fondly her loyalty to St Benedict's, and in spite of her blunt manner, to Geoff and myself. Whatever had to be done, whether it was brass, or church cleaning, or allowing her home to be used for a house group venue, Gladys could always be relied on.

Though, thankfully, I could not have known it at the time, being able to rely on the support of people like Gladys Eliot was going to become very important to me in the weeks and months to come!

'Almighty God, we thank you for feeding us,' we began the thanksgiving prayer together. As the little service ended, I smiled in satisfaction and turning to Gladys, began:

'Well, Gladys, I'll look in after you've had your operation.'

'Ar, I should 'ope so!' the booming voice cut me short. 'There's others in 'ere could do with a visit, an' all! 'Er over theer's 'ad a bad time!'

She nodded expansively to a thin woman who was trying, unsuccessfully, to hide behind her newspaper away from the curious stares of the other patients and their visitors.

'I remember 'er 'usband from when I kept the "Fox 'n' Dogs"!' Gladys went on, undeterred. ' 'E was the biggest drunkard that ever walked in a pair o' shoes!'

CHAPTER THREE

When I got home at lunchtime, there was a message on the answerphone from Turleys, the local undertakers, to say they had a funeral for me.

'I must've just missed it,' Mark had just come in himself, and was busy making sandwiches.

'As Berkley's always telling us, this is one of the joys of only working one day a week!' Mark replied, when I said how nice it was to enjoy a lunch time snack together.

'He didn't say that when we went to his school though, did he?' I smiled as I remembered my stepson's twelve-year-old face, at once proud and horrified, when not only one but two dog-collared parents were asked to talk to his year group in their 'learning through themes' sessions.

'Well at least he's not following his big brother and talking about becoming a Rastafarian in protest!' Mark grinned as we both thought of sixteen-year-old Edmund, and his penchant for loud music and outlandish ideas.

'Not yet!' I sighed, collecting our plates before making my way to the phone to ring Turleys. 'I wonder if this is anyone we know?'

Steven Turley, whose family had run the

funeral directors in Netherley Bank from time immemorial, gave me the details himself.

'It's a baby, I'm afraid, Carol, ten months old,' he said. 'The parents are Dawn and Wayne Mason, 32, Shakespeare Grove. They've asked for you specially. Apparently you did the baptism.'

I'd baptised Simon Mason a month before. A bonny little boy in a white romper suit, I remembered how he had blinked and looked straight up at me as I splashed the warm water from St Benedict's stone font on his curly dark head. Now, Steven was telling me he was dead. That all that life and warmth had gone.

'I'll go round to Dawn and Wayne's now,' I told Mark after explaining the situation. 'I wonder what on earth could have happened to him?'

As I was quickly discovering, life in parish ministry held daily surprises, not all of them pleasant.

Shakespeare Grove was a row of maisonettes tucked into one of the back streets of the local estate known as Poet's Corner. To reach it, I had to walk past several graffiti-scrawled, boarded-up shops, and a pub which had obviously seen better days.

The whole estate gave off an atmosphere of neglect and apathy. Although there were many hardworking; law-abiding tenants who lived there, there were also many no-hopers. Youngsters often left the local secondary

16

school with no future but to follow their parents onto the dole queue. Like many other places, Netherley Bank had its fair share of the resulting vandalism and petty crime.

I knew for certain that St Benedict's had very few, if any, attenders from this end of the parish. But people like Dawn and Wayne Mason, married or single, still brought their babies to the great church on the hill to be baptised.

'Reverend Carol.' Wayne's thin, pale face relaxed momentarily as he opened the door of the maisonette. 'Come in.' Ordering an enthusiastic collie dog into the kitchen, he called, 'It's the lady from the church, Dawn!'

Her long, dark hair streaming down her shoulders, Dawn Mason looked up at me from the sofa. Although no more than twenty-two, the age of my own daughter, she seemed to have aged twenty years since I saw her at the baptism.

'I got up to fetch him into our room,' she whispered as I sat down and took her icy hand in mine. 'He was usually awake early and talking to himself, not crying, just talking and laughing, but he was so quiet and I picked him up and then I screamed—me babby—me babby! I just kept screaming and Wayne run for the neighbour, and she tried so hard to start him breathing again!'

'Oh, Dawn!' Knowing there was nothing to say, nothing to do except what I would want

17

someone to do for me or for my Sarah in these agonising circumstances, I just held out my arms and she came straight into them.

'I'll put the kettle on,' Wayne said unsteadily, opening the kitchen door. As the collie darted in, desperate to get close to us, Dawn found a tissue and wiped her eyes. 'He don't know what's going on, do you, Patch?' she said. 'He keeps going into Simon's room and looking in the cot.'

'Is that what they think it was, cot death?' I asked gently.

Dawn nodded desolately. 'There's got to be a post mortem, that's why we can't have the service until next week.' Her tear-ravaged eyes met mine as Wayne came back into the room with mugs of tea. 'I want you to do it, please, and I want him to be in his christening suit.'

'Whatever you want is okay by me,' I assured them. 'And I want you to know that we'll all be praying for you at church.' Although the Masons weren't regular members of our congregation, I knew their plight would touch many hearts when I put baby Simon's name on the list of the departed.

'He liked the candle,' Wayne suddenly said, breaking the silence. 'You know, the candle you gave us at the christening? He kept reaching out for it, and laughing.'

I nodded, wishing there was something more I could say to help them. 'Help, Lord!' I prayed, silently, and the answer was there, so obvious it was staring me in the face.

'Have you still got the candle?' I asked quietly, and when Dawn, heaving herself to her feet, got up to fetch it; 'Let's light it now, shall we? Just to thank God for Simon, and to ask him to take good care of him, and you, over the next few days?'

When I got home, Mark was getting ready for one of his ladies class meetings. With four chapels to care for in the circuit, and invitations from neighbouring circuits, he was kept pretty busy giving talks.

Briefly, I told him about my sad funeral visit.

'Maybe you should put them in touch with Ruth Walters at the hospital,' he suggested, giving me a supportive hug. 'Or is it just neo-natal deaths she deals with?'

'No.' I thought of my fellow priest, and hospital chaplain, Revd Ruth. In the sunlit chapel at Russets Road she had made a private corner, surrounded by panels of stained glass, where a bereaved mother could sit and rock her stillborn baby's body, wrapped tenderly in tiny clothes and laid in a beautiful wicker Moses basket. 'She arranges counselling sessions and memorial services for anyone who's lost a child, however old, and however long ago.'

After he had left, I went up to my study and gave Ruth a ring.

'The important thing is just to be available if

19

and when they want to talk, Carol,' she said, in her no-nonsense Northern voice. 'Pop in next time you're on the wards and I'll let you have details of the support scheme we have here. And don't forget, if there's anything I can do . . .'

'Thanks, Ruth.' I put the phone down feeling marginally more equipped to deal with baby Simon's funeral, and the pastoral care of his young parents, knowing it was something I wouldn't have to attempt alone.

Now, though, I realised with a start, looking at my watch, it was more than time I started the spaghetti Bolognese for tea!

I was in the kitchen busily chopping onions when the telephone rang.

'Carol?' said Geoff's familiar voice. 'Is anything wrong?'

I gulped down the tears. 'No, just onions,' I half lied. 'I'm fine.'

'Good!' The relief in my colleague's voice should have warned me. 'Look, I hate to ask you this, but Jane's just come home from work with the most terrible migraine, which means I'll have to fetch the girls from school. Could I ask you to do the confirmation class at Encounter this afternoon?'

Like many activities in and around St Benedict's, Encounter had been started by a previous curate and never discontinued. It consisted of up to twenty ten to twelve-year-olds who met every week to play games, let off steam, and hopefully learn something of the

Christian gospel. Those who were taking the confirmation classes should, hopefully, be confirmed by the bishop next spring.

Agreeing to stand in for Geoff, I tidied the kitchen ready for the next stage of spaghetti Bolognese preparation. Then I scrubbed my fingers with lemon juice, scribbled Mark a note, sorted out my youth work folder, and set off.

As I walked down the busy High Street towards the parish centre, I reflected on the brightness of the day. Netherley Bank wasn't a bad place to be on a summer afternoon, with the trees in the coppice in bloom, and roses in profusion in people's front gardens.

Halfway down, the High Street was transformed as if by a time machine, to another age. There were shops there that hadn't changed for thirty years, and no one seemed to want them to.

There were rusting chewing gum machines outside the low, wide shop windows, and inside, bare shelves that spoke of almost wartime austerity. The shoe shop was museum-like, as was the chemist's, while the barber's shop had a hole in the roof. But the smell from the Netherley Bank chippy was something not easily described in words, and as I hurried along I realised, my mouth watering, that lunch seemed a long time ago.

When I reached the red brick parish centre, there was already a little crowd waiting outside. Half of them disbanded, and gathered round me.

'What we doin' tonight, miss?'

'C'n me and Julie sell the sweets, miss?'

'Hey, miss, my little sister said you come to 'er school last wick!'

While the boys pretended disinterest, scuffling along on the edge of the pavement, the girls vyed with one another to link arms with me.

'Thought it was Geoff for the confirmation lot today?' I looked up with relief as Sally Watkins, the daughter of Mary, one of our church wardens, got out of her car and came towards me. She helped with Encounter most weeks.

Handing one of the bigger boys my key to the centre, I explained about Jane's migraine. Then I helped Sally unload her equipment, including the boxes of lollipops, chewing gum and red liquorice strips.

By the time we were all seated in a circle the other helper, Cindy Taylor, had arrived, and I felt able to cream off the five very assorted children who were this year's confirmation candidates. One face was particularly welcome.

'Michelle!' I exclaimed, as we sat in a corner of the stage listening to someone thump the ancient piano, while another group played a noisy game of 'bulldog'. 'Where have you been? I haven't seen you in church for ages!'

Michelle Jacques was a pretty twelve-year-old with a peaches and cream complexion. Up until last year, she had been the leading light at St Benedict's rather static Sunday School, her mother an active member of the church.

Now, she looked from her giggling friends to me, her face almost regally disdainful. 'Sorry, miss,' she said airily, 'but I 'ad a boyfriend, see. An' yo' know what it's like, when yo'm courtin' strong!'

As I blinked, and tried to take this in, she suddenly reached across and patted my arm: 'It's all right, I've packed him in now,' she consoled me. And then, with one of those amazing back flips from going-on-twenty-five to just-turned-twelve, she gave an excited gasp:

'Hey, miss, when we've finished talkin' about Jesus, can we play "murder in the dark"?'

As I said before, life in parish ministry holds many surprises!

CHAPTER FOUR

Tom Jenkins was beginning one of his stories. 'There's this widder down our road, see, vicar, an' 'er's bin courtin' a bloke for twenty years!'

'Yes, Tom.' I was taking off my chasuble after the Tuesday evening Eucharist. As usual, Tom had acted as sacristan at the altar, his movements slow and mechanical, but perfectly in tune.

'Well, t'other day, 'e was comin' ter see 'er when 'e sid summat a glitterin' on the pavement, like!' Tom's eager fingers held out a medal, silver-coloured and stamped with an emblem. 'St Benedict's bi-centenary, 1977.'

'So 'e knocked at our door an' 'e said to my Daisy, is Mr Jenkins in, cause 'e knowed who it belonged to!'

I looked at the medal before signing my name in the service book. 'Lost it, had you, Tom?'

'Ar!' Tom's wizened face came closer. 'Good job 'e knowed we. See, my Daisy an' 'is misses was confined together!'

As I tried to think of a suitable reply, Michael, one of the altar boys, put in: 'Why, what'd they done?'

Tom tutted expressively: 'When they 'ad their *babbies*, yer mawkin!'

'These kids!' he snorted after Michael,

grinning, had gone. 'They dow know nuthin'. Good job yo'm a girl o' the cloth, vicar, or I'd say what I really think on 'em!'

'You can anyway,' I said, as I led the way out of the vestry. 'I was coming to see you and Daisy this evening.'

As Tom and I walked down the High Street, he began to tell another story. This time it was about how he met an old friend in the shopping precinct at Merrily Mall the week before.

It started, typically, in the trenches of the first world war, where Tom's elder brother had served with his old friend's second cousin. It lasted right up until he put the key in the front door of his terraced house and admitted me into the surprised and delighted embrace of Daisy.

'Ow am yer, darlin'?' Daisy was as round as Tom was long and thin. Eighty if she was a day, she wore bright red lipstick and vivid clothes that contrasted with her pink rinsed grey hair.

A 'dresser' in the long gone days of local theatre, she always made sure Tom sported a homemade tie in the same material as her frocks.

'Not such a bobby-dazzler as you, Daisy,' I said, as she kissed me again. 'What've you been up to, then?'

'Just recovering the three piece,' she explained, modestly waving a heavily beringed

25

hand. The three piece, blue last time I called, was now a marvel in pin-tucked pink velour.

'Try it out while I put the kettle on! An' you'll 'ave a piece of my gattox?'

Daisy's 'gattox', brimming with cream, resplendent in pink icing like a fairytale castle, was the talk of the parish.

Sinking into the velour sofa, pressed by Tom to accept extra cushions, I gave myself up to the luxury of forgetting all about my diet.

As we ate, we talked, or rather, Tom and Daisy talked, and I listened. They had five grown-up children, countless grandchildren, and four tiny great grandchildren, all of whom came to visit every Sunday afternoon.

'It's no wonder we dow often mek it to evensong, darlin',' Daisy said, ruefully, as she refilled my teacup from a huge, floral china pot. 'But still, yer family's yer family, ay it?'

They both looked so well, so full of life, I could scarcely believe it when, early the next morning, Geoff telephoned me with the news that Tom had been rushed into hospital during the night.

'Suspected heart attack,' he said. 'It sounds as if he's in a pretty bad way.'

I found Tom in the intensive care unit of Russets Road. He was silent and motionless, his eyes closed, and attached to several frightening-looking machines.

'We're not sure he's going to make it,' the doctor I asked told me, bluntly. 'It was a massive coronary, and his age is against him.'

Poor Tom! I sat for ages at his bedside. The comforting words of several psalms came into my mind, and as I anointed him with holy oil, I whispered: 'Keep him as the apple of your eye, Lord. Hide him beneath the shadow of your wings.'

I turned my head as a movement came at my side. Daisy was there, the bright scarf at her neck belying the pallor of her face. A face that suddenly for the first time looked its age.

'It's the fust night we've ever bin apart, darlin' except fer when the babbies was born,' she said, unsteadily. 'I allus tode 'im—Tommy Jenkins, I couldn't live without yer . . .!'

'Let's hope you won't have to, Daisy,' I tried to say encouragingly. 'Come and sit down. Hold his other hand, and we'll have a prayer together.'

The next morning, I popped in to see Tom again, and was amazed to see him sitting up in bed! He was, so Daisy told me in a stage whisper, 'being took off the danger list,' but still had to take things easily.

'The next 'un might be fatal, so it's no more gattox fer 'im, darlin!' she told me firmly, enfolding me into her perfumed, cushioned embrace. 'That was a warning, the doctor said.'

As I looked at the white-haired figure in the bed, I realised resignedly that this was going to mean the end of a lot of activities for Tom

Jenkins, and, by extension, radical changes at St Benedict's.

Just then, Tom looked up and caught my eye. 'No more chasin' ferrets, eh, vicar!' he said, regretfully. Then he yawned and stretched, glad to be alive. And automatically began to tell another story.

'Know me? Well, I got three pairs o' trousers, see . . . ?'

CHAPTER FIVE

'The peace of God, which passes all understanding keep your hearts and minds in the knowledge and love of God, and of his son, Jesus Christ our Lord, and the blessing . . .'

I made the sign of the cross over St Benedict's gathered congregation at the end of the Sunday morning Eucharist, and prepared to be blasted out by Clarke's swelling 'amen' chord after the dismissal.

As usual, the choir, comprising ten middle-aged women and three stalwart men, lined up in twos to genuflect to the high altar before the grand recessional into the vestry. They had been in fine voice that morning, and I complimented them on their singing.

'I wondered if Clarke would be able to play with that bandage on his finger,' Brenda Mountback said, wide-eyed with curiosity, as she took off her red robe. 'What on earth's he been doing?'

Brenda, our leading contralto, had become a special friend, mainly through my visits to her housebound mother, Eliza.

Before I could answer her question, the vestry door opened and Clarke himself swept in. Ignoring me, he addressed the choir en masse. 'There's an extra practice tonight before choral Evensong. Five forty-five, sharp.

I expect everyone to be here!'

It was Geoff's turn for Evensong, and I couldn't help but be glad as I later made my way back to the manse for lunch. Our Sundays were always hectic, and this one was particularly so, with a meeting that afternoon with our suffragan Bishop Paul, and other local clergy to discuss possible weekly services for the Sunday shoppers at Merrily Mall.

'Well, if they won't come to us, we have to do a John Wesley and go to them,' Mark grinned, as he mixed the gravy.

'Do a who?' I teased, returning from helping the boys to set the table. Privately, I thought it an excellent idea to take the gospel to where people were. Shopping, whether it was in the enormous American style centre, or just at local car boot sales, seemed to have replaced Sunday worship in many people's lives, a situation which of course kept many others rejoicing all the way to the bank.

The meeting, held at a newly re-ordered church building on the outskirts of Merrily Mall, was attended by representatives of many local churches, and several denominations.

After a brief introduction by Bishop Paul, the Revd Derrick Jones, the Mall's industrial chaplain, outlined the scheme that was being suggested. Short, regular services, conducted on a rota basis, in the central arena.

'Sunday afternoons seem the obvious time,' he said, in his rather worried, lilting Welsh voice, as several clergy groaned aloud. 'At about two-thirty, so as to not interfere with our morning services, and to give us a chance to get back for the evening ones!'

'Great idea, kid!' Revd Mervyn Mitchell, the rural dean, looked up perkily from the contemplation of his diary and clicked his fingers. 'Something snappy and accessible, that's what we need. Half an hour the shoppers won't forget!'

'That's precisely what I'm afraid of, Father!' As the condescending voice rose from the back of the meeting, I turned my head. Revd Brian Stanway, incumbent of St Aloysius', our neighbouring parish, had risen to his feet, looking pale with displeasure. 'Our holy mother church is not in the entertainment business,' he pointed out, vehemently. 'We have already seen what havoc is wreaked when she bows to the whims and passing trends of the age!'

'I think,' said Mark, sotto voce to me, as the turbulent priest resumed his seat amid grunts and mutters. 'You're supposed to be one of the whims and passing trends!'

'Mmmmm.' I'd already encountered Father Brian at clergy chapter meetings. Marching into the room, he would intone 'Good morning, brothers!' so pointedly that I squirmed. Once the ordination of the first women priests had taken place, he and the whole of St Aloysius had announced they would soon be sheltering under the wings of a flying bishop!

When the meeting was adjourned, it being decided to form a sub committee to arrange the rota, there was a sudden flurry by the door.

'Ah, the press photographer!' Bishop Paul beamed, getting to his feet. 'The diocesan communications officer thought it might be rather good to get this in the local paper—let people know we're planning something.'

'I don't think we need hang around for this, do we?' I whispered to Mark, one eye on the door. 'We've still got to collect the boys from Sarah's, and get ready for your evening service.'

But the photographer, spotting my dog collar, obviously had other ideas. 'A woman priest!' he said, eyes lighting up as he caught me by the arm. 'Great! Now you just stand here, love, get some of these gentlemen around you.'

The bishop, Mark, Derrick and Mervyn were soon obediently taking up the positions they had been given, while the photographer looked quickly around for a fifth.

'Great!' he said again, as I met Mark's eyes, torn in that moment between the desire to laugh and cry. 'You're the one I want, mate! You—you by the door, in the dress!'

Father Brian's shudder reverberated like a tidal wave through the room. 'No way!' he exploded, allowing himself one apoplexied, horrified glance in my direction. 'I am

32

extremely sorry, but I could not possibly be seen in public with . . . !'

'It's like I've got the plague!' I had been through it all before, and yet I still stormed, full of pain and righteous indignation as Mark and I drove home.

Fury crashed through me as I thought of the injustice of it all. 'If I were—say—a midwife, and we had a male midwife who'd trained with us, I'd recommend him not marginalise him! I'd admire him for his courage!'

My lovely husband reached out a hand to comfortingly squeeze my fingers. 'Ah, but the brothers aren't like you—that's why you've got 'em running scared,' he said, and then, with his familiar, mischievous twinkle: 'Now, if only you'd been sensible, and joined the one, true church. We Methodists know how to treat our lady ministers!'

As Mark's superintendent minister, his immediate superior in the circuit, was a woman, there wasn't much I could say about that!

Pushing Father Brian's latest snub to the back of my mind, I began to think of the more important matter of little Simon Mason's funeral, looming on the horizon of the following day.

Monday was, despite the time of year, a grey and rainy day. After lunch, I put on my black cassock early, making sure that the newly pressed surplice, purple stole and funeral book were ready to hand. The moment the funeral cars drew up outside, I clipped on my heavy black cloak, remembering to check that I had the house keys, a comb, and a little emergency change in my possession.

I had already discovered that priests look silly carrying handbags, apart from the fact that there is never anywhere to put them. So I was very grateful for my capacious cassock pockets.

Steven Turley deferentially opened the door of the hearse for me. A slight, bespectacled man whose appearance and bearing were very much in keeping with his profession, Steve was a committed Christian and a lay reader at his own church. He was well known in the area for providing spiritual as well as practical support for the families who came to him.

'We'll have to say a lot of prayers for this one, Carol,' he said as we both looked back at the flower strewn coffin, so incongruously tiny in the hearse. 'No matter how often we get them, I never quite get used to babies dying.'

The rain was pouring down by the time we had driven the mile to Netherley Bank crematorium. A building which looked from a distance as if it were made of glass-coated lego, it sat in the middle of an oasis of flower beds and rose gardens which today were water-logged and uninviting.

As was the customary practice, I left the hearse as soon as it stopped, hurrying under the canopy to make sure everything was ready in the chapel. As I did so, I offered up a quick prayer of thanks that it looked as if there would be no waiting around, which could sometimes happen if the crematorium was busy.

Dawn and Wayne were almost unrecognisable in their severe black clothes, as Steve and his attendants helped them in. As the organist began to play I led the procession, with Steve carrying the little coffin, and my heart was really full.

Before the opening prayer, both sets of parents, Simon's grandparents, came forward to hug and kiss the brave young couple. The gesture said so much about the solidarity of this working class, Black Country family. It was the kind of family I had been lucky enough to be brought up in myself, where blood really was thicker than water, and people genuinely knew what it meant to bear each other's burdens. The family of the church could well take a pattern from the Christlike love of so-called unchurched families like this, I thought, recalling briefly the meeting of the day before.

As the congregation rose to sing the solitary hymn, 'All things bright and beautiful,' my every ounce of mingled empathy and admiration was up and running. I had to remind myself swiftly of all we had been taught in theological training.

I was at Simon Mason's funeral in a special

role, my job to keep control, and to also free his stricken family to grieve in this very important rite of passage. And just as always, God was right there, giving me all the strength and composure I needed, to do what had to be done.

CHAPTER SIX

At our weekly staff meeting Geoff and I worked, as usual, through our diaries, deciding who would be responsible for what commitment.

'We're due at Willow Tree nursing home at three,' he said, chewing his pen thoughtfully, 'but we've also got the mixed infants coming into church.'

'That's okay. I can see to the children then meet you for communion at the home,' I suggested. 'It's really hot, so we won't be able to keep either group concentrating too long!'

The rain of the day before had done nothing to cool the air, and as I later made my way across the busy road, I sweltered in my dog-collared shirt. It would be good before lunch to walk with Mark, and Becky and Gran, our much loved family mongrels, in the coppice. Gran at seventeen years old was quite a character, and we used tales of her antics, real and imaginary, to illustrate our weekly assemblies at St Benedict's primary.

A little group of St Benedict's pupils passed me as I walked through the gates of the manse. Some faces were familiar from Sunday School or Rainbows, others were seen less regularly at family weddings or the baptisms of younger siblings.

A chorus of friendly, 'Hello, Mrs 'Athorne!' met me and I grinned as I walked down the path and opened the front door. Many of the smaller local children had their own version of our unusual surname, and as I walked over the threshold, Mark called from his study:

'Hello, Mrs Acorn!'

'Hello, Mr Acorn!' I replied, giving him a kiss. 'I was just thinking we should take to the woods and give the dogs an airing before I go back to church to show the infants round!'

His afternoon schedule was as busy as mine, but we did have a short time to spare for what had become not only our exercise but our battery recharging time.

Although the traffic was only a few hundred yards away, God always seemed very close in the peace and quiet of Netherley Bank coppice. While Becky bounded ahead, investigating every bush and interesting tree stump, Gran padded majestically after us, her tail wagging slowly as she stopped now and then to catch her breath and nibble on some medicinal grass stalks.

As we walked, two figures hand in hand in clerical collars, we talked about many things—the problems of individual members of our congregations, the sermons we would be preaching on Sunday. The adjustments already made, and still being made within our new, extended family. A family which contained not only two ministers of different Christian denominations, but three stepchildren, one of whom had had the luxury of growing up as an only child.

A whole lot of prayer had gone on behind the scenes during the twelve months since our wedding day, and much of it in this lovely, ancient place.

After lunch, I crossed the road again just as a straggling crocodile of children came up the High Street. They were soon assembled in a noisy throng near our ornate baptistry.

When arranging the visit, their teachers, Mrs Cox and Mrs Leckings, had suggested they might be shown what happens at a christening, wedding, and funeral.

With the assistance of 'Rebecca', my daughter's long discarded baby doll, I demonstrated how a baby is baptised.

'I expect many of you were baptised here at St Benedict's,' I said, as they came forward, pushing one another in their eagerness to peer into the Victorian font. 'I know I've baptised some of your baby brothers and sisters.'

Immediately, I was met with a chorus of raised hands and voices:

'Missis 'Afforne—you done my baby!'

'An' my bruther!'

'An', an' my cousin, Missis Acorn!'

Clapping her hands, Mrs Cox called: 'That's enough! Let Mrs Hathorne tell us about baptising Rebecca!'

As the hubbub died down, I wrapped the

realistic looking doll closer in its shawl and held it over the font, describing how God was going to give the baby a special blessing and make her a member of his family, and how her parents must make extra special promises to teach her about Jesus.

'Now we're all going to walk—very, very slowly, and without saying a word, right down the aisle of this lovely church,' I said, after I'd finished the mock baptism. 'Because we're going to take baby Rebecca up to the high altar, to thank God for all he's done for her.'

Mrs Leckings raised her eyebrows when I asked for the silence and there was a certain amount of clamour as the youngsters were put back into their crocodile.

'Now, as you walk, I want you to remember all the babies who have been carried, like Rebecca here, down this aisle in nearly a hundred and fifty years,' I said, thanking God for the gradually rapt faces, the change in atmosphere that the silence brought. 'I want you to think, too, of all the beautiful ladies who have walked down it on their wedding day, and the people who have died, who have come here for their sad friends to say goodbye.'

Carefully carrying the doll, I led the procession slowly down the aisle which echoed as always with the memory of other acts of worship, reverberating for me with the breath of the communion of souls.

As I held Rebecca up to the altar, I felt rather than saw a handful of the mostly unchurched children of Netherley Bank, come to the communion rail and silently kneel as if in spontaneous homage to the Christ Child some of them had scarcely heard about.

It was one of the most moving moments in my ministry so far, and I caught the surprised and gratified glances of the two teachers.

After that, it was easy to talk to them, squashed into the choir stalls, about other things that went on in church: the Sunday services where, when you were old enough, you could sing in the choir, ring the bells, or learn to serve at the altar; the Sunday School that was always on the look out for new members.

'Missis 'Athrne?' I asked for questions, and immediately the hands shot up again. 'What's all the candles for?'

Rosie, a little girl with a face like a cabbage patch doll who always looked as if she was wearing an older sister's clothes, nodded shyly to the candle stand beneath the pulpit.

'Well,' I explained, 'here at St Benedict's we light candles when we want to say a prayer for someone who's poorly, or in trouble. On Sundays, there's usually a candle alight on every one of those little ledges.'

As a request came to light a candle for one little boy's grandad in hospital, I encouraged the children to kneel in the first two rows of

41

pews.

'Lord, please help David's grandad when he has his operation,' I prayed, as the light sprang alive.

'Amen,' intoned classes one and two obediently.

'And Alex's mummy, who's having a new baby.'

'And Claire's daddy, with the toothache.'

Fascinated, they joined in with their 'amens' again and again as names and petitions came. I had never had such a spiritually in tune, yet humanely empathetic congregation. No one whispered or talked out of turn; their whole attention focused on those lights and the promise behind and within them.

'Misses 'Athorne?' The raised hands became braver, the offerings for prayer more open, and at the same time, more needy and confused: 'My aunty went to Jesus an' she was in the graveyard 'ere.'

'An' my nan went to Jesus, an' my mommy brought some flowers to her!'

I lit the candles and said the prayers, my heart warming at the relief on some of the small faces. It was a new satisfaction for them, powerless as they were in a grown up world they couldn't understand, to feel they could do something for those they loved.

'I think it's time we stopped now,' Mrs Cox clapped her hands and gently indicated the time.

'Misses 'Athorne!' Jamie, Rosie's brother, called out urgently, his hand in the air. He took a deep breath. 'My dog got runned over an' the vet put some plastic on 'is leg!' he said, hopefully.

'Er, yes, Jamie.' As I lit the candle, I realised Mrs Cox was right. It was definitely time to stop. Besides, Willow Tree nursing home was waiting.

CHAPTER SEVEN

The nursing home was privately run, and operated from what used to be the doctor's house. A large, Georgian building, it had been much extended at the back, with small, ultra modern bedrooms leading off hushed and carpeted corridors. In the centre was a lounge with a television set at each end, and hunched, immobile figures in armchairs lining the walls.

Walking past the owner's red Porsche standing in pride of place on the forecourt, I rang the doorbell. 'I've come to help with the service,' I explained, as a large girl in a white nylon overall undid the chain and let me in.

Though we visited Willow Tree every month, our arrival always seemed to be met with a vague surprise and suspicion, as if, despite the entry in the diary, they'd forgotten all about us.

I found Geoff standing in the middle of the lounge, with the four lady members of St Benedict's congregation who always came along to support the event. He looked very relieved to see me.

'Right!' With a flourish, my colleague produced from his briefcase a cassette tape. He beamed around the apathetic lounge in the manner of one about to bestow a priceless gift. 'I have here a recording of hymns made on

Sunday by St Benedict's church choir, specially for our nursing home services!'

As the helpers, now busy giving out the battered hymn books, looked impressed, the residents of Willow Tree nursing home drew suspiciously back in their armchairs. Some were asleep, some muttered mutinously about the television sets being turned off. Somewhere in the kitchen far away, the staff were talking and occasionally letting out peals of laughter.

'Here at Willow Tree,' Geoff went on, as I passed him the portable cassette player from my own briefcase, 'we have the privilege of hearing the tape for the very first time, so you could say that we're making history!'

He inserted the tape into the machine and pressed the play button. There came the sound of a commanding voice, a tap of a baton, a cough, and then finally the strains of 'Love Divine'.

As Geoff and I and the helpers joined in, a couple of quavering voices were lifted: 'All thy faithful mercies crown.'

'Great!' Geoff exclaimed, encouraged, as the hymn ended. 'I'm going to ask Reverend Carol to say a prayer for us now, then you'll get another chance to sing.'

He sat down, mopping his brow, and I asked if there was anyone ill in hospital or at the home, in special need of our prayers. There was little response, so I offered a prayer of thanksgiving for the lovely summer weather, and then asked God's blessing on all at Willow Tree nursing home, residents, staff and visitors alike.

'Our Father,' I concluded, and felt a little buzz of gratitude and well-being as even the most seemingly distant members of our sadly captive congregation suddenly came to life and joined in. 'Hallowed be thy name.'

Whatever else they forgot, even those suffering with severe dementia seemed always able, in my experience, to remember the words of not only the Lord's Prayer, but the hymns they had been taught in childhood. I remembered an old lady in hospital, who had kept the whole ward awake all night shouting gibberish and seemed to recognise no one and understand nothing. Then she had spotted me in my cassock and, her cloudy eyes suddenly crackling recognition, had caught at my hand. She began to rock backwards and forwards, happily croaking: 'What a friend we have in dar-dar, all our dar-dar-dar-dar-dar!'

'Next hymn then!' Geoff got enthusiastically to his feet and turned back to the cassette player. 'All people that on earth do dwell!' There came again a command, coughs and splutters before the Old Hundred drifted out of the little player.

Our stalwart helpers went round flicking open hymn books, pointing to words, consoling the confused, or those who could not see to read the words. A moment later, the anthem began to swell, and I turned to my colleague and nodded. We really seemed to be getting somewhere today, despite the age and state of the congregation. Despite the disinterested atmosphere of the surroundings. Despite, even, the crippling heat of the day.

'We really know this one!' Geoff burst out, catching the mood. He waved his black shirt sleeved arms in the air: 'Sing up! Sing up!'

In their memories, I thought returning to my daydreams, there must surely be Sunday School processions where they'd sat on chapel platforms in white dresses as this old hymn was sung.

Lost in my thoughts, I didn't at first notice the big girl in the white nylon overall. Coming out of the kitchen, she stopped in the middle of the lounge, a large carrier bag clutched to her ample bosom.

Heat rose in the lounge, battling with the bravely struggling old voices: 'Come ye before him and rejoice!'

As we took a deep breath between verses, the girl began to deftly unwrap something from the bag. Going quickly and expertly from armchair to armchair, she popped an object into each conveniently open mouth.

'Oh no! Just as we'd got them going!' Geoff muttered to me as we stared from each other to the amazing sight in front of us, trying not to burst out laughing.

47

Afterwards, in his most polite 'vicar's voice' he said: 'Well, perhaps next time we come to Willow Tree nursing home, if we're very good, *we'll* get an iced lollipop, too!'

CHAPTER EIGHT

'Ar, our Brenda's always been a good singer,' Eliza Smart said, with a sigh of quiet satisfaction. 'When I used to get home from the brickworks, tired out and riffy, it used to do my heart good, to hear her, trillin' away in the entry!'

It always seemed impossible that dainty Eliza, with her neat cap of snow white hair and bird bright brown eyes had ever been capable of the physically demanding manual labour at the now defunct factory where furnace bricks had been made.

Nearly ninety now, she lived alone in the two up, two down house where she and her long dead steelworker husband had raised a family of six sons and one daughter. The daughter, our contralto Brenda Mountback, was the only one who still lived close enough to pop in and keep an eye on Eliza, something the old lady always staunchly insisted was absolutely unnecessary.

'Waste not, want not' was Eliza's watchword. On my every visit, she'd show me something new that had come out of her old fashioned Black Country resourcefulness.

Today was no exception. While I sat opposite her, enjoying the cup of tea and slice of homemade cake she always produced at the end of our prayer time, she suddenly thrust her small feet in my direction:

'Like the way I mended me shoes?'

I inspected the beige coloured flatties, remembering how I'd warned her the sole was beginning to flap on the right one and she should, for safety's sake, ask Brenda to get her a new pair. 'They look safer, anyway. What did you use, superglue?'

Eliza shook her snowy head. She made me wait, enjoying herself. 'Chewing gum!' she finally supplied. 'Our Tommy's lad come to see me the other day and left a strip of it behind, so I thought, now what can I use this for?'

'But . . .' The picture of little Eliza going round the house grimly chewing to make shoe glue was irresistible. Only one thing puzzled me. 'Didn't it stick to your teeth?'

'Course not!' Eliza shook her head again as if the answer were obvious. 'I always take them out to eat with!' she explained. 'A bit of spearmint's no problem, when yo've got gums as good as mine!

'Anyroadup, my lover,' she went on a few moments later, 'that's enough about my antics! I'm going to take you in the garden before you go home and we'll pick some roses.'

Eliza's roses, planted long ago by her late husband Harold, were her pride and joy. Every summer she wasted none of them, sharing them with friends, neighbours and even strangers who happened to walk by and

50

admire the bright display.

'First we have to cut off the thorns!' Later, back in her dark kitchen, I stood and watched as Eliza's spritely, work-worn fingers closed over the scissors she'd mended with electrician's masking tape, and deftly snipped away all the pale, spiky thorns. 'If you get them in your fingers, yo'll know about it, my wench!'

A moment later, she put the scissors down and laid the roses on the table. Darting to a carrier bag hanging on the back of the pantry door, she pulled a mishmash of re-cycled wrapped papers, crumpled and smoothed and crumpled again, and along with them, a handful of multi-coloured wool strips, safety pins, baby ribbon and string. 'Now we'll lap 'em up all fancy for yer!'

My visits to Eliza, as much of spiritual benefit to me as to her, always took longer than I anticipated, and when I came out of her gate and turned into the High Street, I found the familiar figure of Berkley, my stepson, winging towards me on his bike.

'I've come to see you across the road, Cazza,' he said, drawing to a breathtaking skid at my side, 'being as you nearly got run over the other day.'

'I day!' I protested in the local dialect, though secretly delighted at his concern. Taking on two lively boys hadn't been without its traumas and I was thankful for each small reward as it came.

51

Berkley pushed back the fair hair that no matter how he plastered it with water always sprang back into curls. 'Yo did!' he said. 'Now hurry up or I'll miss "Star Trek". Andy and Sarah've just come!'

At the manse, the whole of our 'blended' human and animal family was assembled. Sixteen-year-old Edmund, complete with his latest Mohican style haircut, practised death-defying skateboard manoeuvres in the garden while the old dog, Gran, watched complacently from beneath the spreading honeysuckle bush.

Sarah made tea in the kitchen while her husband Andy prepared to squirt Berkley with a loaded water gun as part of their ongoing water fight.

'Aargh!' As Berkley screamed, Becky as usual began jumping up and down barking at the top of her voice to defend him. Meanwhile Jacob, the Siamese cat, darted between my ankles and took refuge upstairs. With a loud thud, he disappeared into the airing cupboard.

'What *is* going on in here?' Eventually, the noise brought Mark from his study, where he had been choosing hymns for his Sunday services.

He stood with his arm around me, surveying the scene, a quiet good-natured man who, thankfully, was not short of a tolerant sense of humour.

As the kitchen door banged and Andy and Berkley disappeared into the garden to continue the fight and annoy Edmund, we carried the tea into the living room.

'Peace at last!' I sighed, kicking off my shoes. 'Now tell us, Sarah, how's the nursery been this week?'

Sarah's job as a nursery nurse in Birmingham often gave us a chuckle, as well as the occasional germ of a sermon idea.

She was halfway through the account of how one toddler decided to smear the nursery bathroom and herself in zinc and castor oil cream when the doorbell suddenly jangled and both dogs set up a loud barking.

'I'll go,' I said, getting to my feet. Closing the door on the noise, I went into the hall and opened the front door.

A thin, balding. man in his fifties stood there, a look of deep anxiety on his pale face. 'Oh, I, er, wasn't expecting a lady,' he mumbled, and then, to my consternation, broke down in tears.

'I'm sorry, so sorry,' he said, as I drew him into the cool quietness of the front room. 'It's just that, well, we were married at St Benedict's twenty-five years ago to the day, this coming Saturday.'

'Oh?' Something stopped me from expressing my congratulations, and I was glad it did, for a moment later, our unexpected visitor explained.

'My wife, Ada, died three months ago, and there's something I want to do for her. My name's Bob Grainger, by the way.'

Over a cup of tea, Bob explained that he and Ada had always planned to return to St Benedict's on their silver wedding anniversary.

'At exactly twelve o'clock—that's the time we got married—I'd planned to bring her into church and ask the vicar for a blessing. Then we were going out for the day, just us and the boys.'

Sadly, Ada had contracted stomach cancer earlier that year, her condition deteriorating rapidly until her death. So Bob had been unable to fulfil his anniversary promise.

'So I wondered, er, Reverend, if it would be possible, in the circumstances, for you to bury Ada's ashes in the garden of remembrance at twelve o'clock on Saturday,' he asked. 'I've had them kept specifically for that purpose.'

He looked so forlorn and yet so hopeful as he pulled a crumpled white handkerchief out of his pocket that my heart went out to him. I was glad he had 'the boys', even though he did seem a little middle-aged to be the father of a young family.

'You really need to contact the undertakers, Bob,' I explained. 'They don't normally do burials on a Saturday round here, but if you tell them I'm willing to officiate there shouldn't be any problem.'

'That's really great.' His thin face filled with relief as he looked up at me over the mug of tea. 'I wasn't sure you'd be able to do it in case you had weddings.'

'I don't have any in my diary,' I said, remembering a plan Sarah and I had made to go shopping on Saturday afternoon, 'but I will ring my colleague just to check, before you leave.'

Going into the study, I quickly rang the vicarage. There was no answer for ages, and I was just about to put the phone down when Jane's rather breathless voice came on the other end.

'St Benedict's vicarage.'

'Hi, Jane,' I said, breezily, 'only me. Can I have a quick word with Geoff, please?'

To my surprise, there was an obviously embarrassed silence. Then Jane said, all in a rush, 'Er, he's not here today, Carol. Sorry.'

Not there. I frowned. Geoff and I made a practice at our staff meetings to synchronise our diaries. Working so closely, it was imperative each should know the other's engagements. He certainly hadn't said anything to me about being out of the parish today, a normal, busy Saturday.

'Oh. Okay.' Jane's obviously guarded manner had me hearing warning bells again, though I naturally couldn't tell her that. 'Would you do me a favour, then? Check and make sure he doesn't have a wedding booked for twelve o'clock on Saturday?'

CHAPTER NINE

Geoff seemed in an efficient mood that Sunday morning. By the time I walked through the vestry door, he was robed ready to take the service and had the servers and choir preparing to line up for the opening procession.

'Sorry you couldn't get me yesterday, Carol,' he said quickly as I hung up my coat. 'Something urgent came up.'

'That's okay.' I explained about Bob Grainger and the silver wedding ritual. 'I just didn't want some bride coming through the lych gate to find herself face to face with a funeral party!'

Whatever Geoff was keeping to himself would, I was sure, be brought into the open when he was sure it was the right time. My worst fear was he was looking for another job, a situation which would leave me to run the parish of twelve thousand souls alone.

As the week went by, I tried to alternately ignore my feelings of unease, and to pray about them. The second course of action was the easiest because I could share it not only with God, but with Mark, when we said Evening Prayer together.

'I think you should listen to those warning bells you keep talking about, darling,' my wise husband said, as we sat in the candlelit front room that Friday evening. 'If there is a possibility that Geoff's got itchy feet, you really need to think about what you might come up against in an interregnum.'

'Mmmm.' I studied his handsome, bearded profile thoughtfully. 'Well, with Tom Jenkins and Gladys Eliot both out of action, we're already at a disadvantage,' I said, 'but I do see signs of hope in other directions.'

Hope was what I intended talking quietly about to Bob Grainger and his boys the next morning. Our wonderful hope in Jesus that Ada was celebrating the anniversary in heaven, all her pain and suffering long over.

I was glad when I set out to cross the High Street that the weather was fine. It was a bright, sunny day with just a hint of autumnal mist around the trees in the coppice.

As I walked, my black cloak flowing behind me, two cars went by, the first a dark green mini, the second Steven Turley's familiar black limousine.

By the time I reached the lych gate, Steven, respectful as usual in his funereal black, stood waiting for me, the tiny coffin of ashes, covered with a small purple cloth, in his hand. At his side, his thin face even paler than I remembered, stood the widower dressed in a smart grey suit and tie, but completely alone.

'Where's your family, Bob?' I asked, as we rather formally shook hands. 'Aren't the boys coming?'

'Oh yes, Reverend. They're waiting in the car.' Turning purposefully on his heel, Bob went back towards the green mini.

At my side, Steven Turley frowned over the casket. 'I don't remember any kids at the funeral, Carol,' he said, sounding puzzled.

We watched in silence as Bob opened the car door and two identical black and white Jack Russell terriers jumped out onto the churchyard tarmac. Clipping them quickly onto leads, Bob brought them, trotting, to where Steven and I stood staring. 'This is Bill and this is Ben,' he said, with loving pride. 'Ada and I never had any other family.'

As Steven, obviously having an uncharacteristic struggle to retain his composure, led the way to the waiting plot in the flower filled garden of remembrance, St Benedict's church clock began to solemnly strike the hour of twelve.

At my side, Bob blinked at me in the suddenly beaming sunshine. 'I knew it would be all right,' he said, gratefully, 'as soon as I rang your doorbell and heard the dogs barking!'

*   *   *

Later that afternoon, I recounted the incident to Sarah as we walked around Dudley market. 'They really are his family,' I said, 'but the thing I'm really pleased about is that he says he's going to start coming to church!'

Just then, something made me look up. Dawn Mason was standing a few yards away from us, a fixed look on her drawn face as she stared at a nearby market stall containing rows and rows of baby clothes.

'Hi, Dawn.' Her face cleared almost guiltily as she started and turned towards us. I introduced Sarah then asked, 'Can I come and see you, say, on Monday?'

The girl nodded. 'Wayne's on lates, so if you come in the afternoon you'll be able to see him an' all.'

'Okay.' After she had gone, hurrying away along the cobbles of the market place, I shook my head worriedly. I had done some hard praying for the Masons since Simon's funeral. Monday morning, without a doubt, I must go into Russets Road and collect that material from my colleague, Ruth.

'Mom!' I came to myself with a jolt, realising Sarah was several yards in front and had turned, glowering, back at me in what had become a familiar way. 'We're supposed to be looking for black leggings. If you don't concentrate, I'm going home!'

When we both finally got home, the black leggings safely discovered, Mark was out taking a wedding, Andy and Berkley were riding bikes on the hill, and Edmund had two messages for me.

59

'One's from a woman called Marcie, about holy water,' he said above the rap music blaring from his room. 'The other's a girl called Stella who says you're doing her wedding next month. Can you ring them both back this evening?'

Later, choosing the easiest first, I rang Stella, a girl who lived just inside the parish with her boyfriend and their three-year-old daughter.

'I was just wondering,' she said, shyly, 'I know we don't come to church or anything, but would it be all right if we had Antonia as our bridesmaid? Only Keith's mom said it wouldn't be allowed as we've done things the wrong way round, like!'

I smiled, remembering Stella from marriage preparation, a bright-eyed, obviously very intelligent young woman who was trying very hard to sort a lot of things out in her own mind. She had asked questions, I remembered, about baptism and marriage. Sacramental questions I felt needed time to be answered.

'I've no objections at all to Antonia being your bridesmaid,' I said. 'It'll make it a very special day for all of you!' What was the point, I thought, of pretending that the child did not exist?

I then rang Marcie Danks, an intense, red-haired woman in her mid-sixties whose paralysed husband Des was one of my sick communicants.

60

'I've run out of holy water, Carol!' she told me, plaintively. 'And I've put it on Des every day since he had his accident. Can you bring some with you when you do the communion on Monday night?'

'I'll try.' As I put down the phone, I wondered about the request. St Benedict's had more than its share of Anglo-Catholics, but holy water wasn't something I was asked for every day.

It was my Sunday off tomorrow, which meant I would be helping Mark with one of his Methodist services. But first, I'd pop into St Benedict's and see Geoff about the holy water before he did his first mass, at nine o'clock. He'd have time to tell me because there wouldn't be many people there.

CHAPTER TEN

Netherley Bank High Street was deserted, only the occasional car breaking the peace of early Sunday morning.

As I walked up the lane towards the great Gothic barn of St Benedict's, I was deep in thought, enjoying the quiet. The view, even from the bottom of Barlow Hill, was quite breathtaking. A multi-faceted landscape spread before me, reading past the spectres of long disused factory chimneys and the hazy countryside of Shropshire on the far horizon.

Going towards the vestry door, I was surprised to see several parked cars on the path around the church. The nine o'clock Book of Common Prayer Eucharist was, I knew from conducting it, one of the least well attended of our services.

Today though, with Geoff on duty, there seemed quite a lot here. Frowning as I went inside, I wondered if it were some special feast day I hadn't heard about. But I already knew from my own readings and preparation that it wasn't.

Why, then, were there at least double the normal congregation? As I sat in the choir stalls, listening to Geoff saying the final prayers of the ancient service, I tried to relax and concentrate on my own private prayers.

But when the congregation stood, I couldn't help but notice, my heart thumping, who was there. Norma and Jim Fisher, as usual sported matching tee shirts emblazoned with 'Jesus is Lord!', and Clarke Pettisgrew, his bearded red face beaming in satisfaction over his smart navy blazer, made it obvious he wasn't there to play the organ.

Many of the others I knew only by sight. But they had one thing in common. They had, as far as I had known until this moment, been missing completely from our church family ever since I had been able to preside at the Eucharist!

Geoff shook hands with them at the vestry door. When the last of them had gone, some almost shamefacedly ignoring me, others nodding in cool politeness before striding self-righteously past into the open air, he turned and looked down at me.

'I'm sorry about that lot, Carol,' he said, regretfully. 'They know I'm one hundred per cent on your side, but they know too they've got a choice of presidents!'

I shook my head, trying not to feel hurt by the memory of the cool stares and tightened lips of some of this hostile congregation.

'We can't force my ministry on them, that's for certain,' I said, 'All we can do is pray that God will find a way to sort out our differences and bind us together again.'

'If it's any consolation,' Geoff replied as he

took off his stole and replaced it carefully in the dresser drawer. 'I've never known a congregation yet that one hundred per cent accepted a priest's ministry. There's always one or two who can't receive communion from him because he's divorced, or gay, or black, or wears an ear-ring.'

'I know,' I said. But as our eyes met, we both realised that what I had just seen was much more than dissent from just one or two opponents of women priests.

My mind was in such a turmoil that I almost forgot the purpose for my being there, to ask Geoff about Marcie Danks' holy water.

He raised his eyebrows, obviously glad to change the subject, but not necessarily to that particular one. 'We really shouldn't encourage this sort of thing you know,' he said, grimly, 'but there is a bottle of Jordan water on the back of the cabinet. Phyllis Evans brought it back from the Holy Land two years ago.'

'Are you sure it's only two years?' As I finally uncovered the small bottle of brackish-looking liquid, I reflected that it seemed much longer since elderly Phyllis went on that package tour to the Holy Land. Hadn't it been nearly two years since, as a deacon, I had helped conduct Phyllis's funeral?

Side stepping the question, Geoff pulled on his jacket and prepared to leave. 'Just tell Marcie to put some salt in it before she uses it,' he instructed me innocently.

Later, over breakfast, I told Mark about my earlier dismay over the nine o'clock service.

'Well, Geoff warned you there might be a split, darling,' he reminded me. 'I suppose you should be grateful they haven't just up and gone to your friend Father Brian. The last I heard of him, he'd dropped off the Merrily Mall service rota on the advice of the flying bishop.'

'What's a flying bishop?' Berkley asked, looking interestedly up from his cereal. 'Does he have a helicopter?'

'No. He's more like Batman than the flying doctor,' I replied. As we finished eating and cleared the table in readiness for Mark's first chapel service of the day, my spirits suddenly lifted. God was everywhere, and no one in the Methodist congregations had turned their noses up at me yet.

Next morning, I made my way to Russets Road hospital to see Revd Ruth in preparation for my afternoon visit to the Masons. I also planned to visit Gladys Eliot and Tom Jenkins who were still laid up there.

A vast, modern complex, the hospital had replaced several smaller, older ones in the district, so that geriatric and psychiatric wings had been built in various stages on the one site.

At one end a long corridor had been constructed, a roomless walk, thickly carpeted and embellished with the modernistic pictures of some fashionable painter. Its purpose was clearly to connect patients to an area of shops, bank and cafeteria which had been tacked onto the hospital complex.

Making my way to the lift, I went up to the fourth floor and the beautiful chapel, which was so different to the converted broom cupboards or cheerless committee rooms offered for some hospital worship.

I stood for a moment in the glow from the stained glass screen, looking at the names on the prayer board, where visitors and patients alike had written their petitions. There was every conceivable message, from the love for a special, terminally ill grandad, to the hope of a cure for a child with leukaemia.

Ruth came in from the wards just as I took a seat in front of the altar. A slim woman of about my own age, she wore a business-like suit over her green clerical shirt, to which was attached a hospital bleeper.

'I've sorted out some material for your young couple,' she said, leading me into her small office. 'There's my card, if they'd like to contact me for a chat, and here's the details for the counselling and the next memorial service. How're they doing, anyway?'

I explained about Dawn's haunted expression in the market place on Saturday. 'She was just staring at the baby clothes stall,' I said, 'almost as if she were in a trance.'

'I expect she is, poor kid.' Ruth sighed and

shook her dark head: 'A lot of the mothers I see talk about living in a fog, especially in the early weeks of losing a child.'

We talked about other cases she had known of what was, sadly, a fairly common tragedy. This area of the Black Country was notoriously high on the list of infant mortality.

'Anyway,' Ruth broke off, grinning, as she glanced at her watch and indicated that it was time for coffee. 'What about you, Carol? What've you been up to since the priesting—chased any old men along corridors lately?'

'No. Not even for a gob-stopper!' As she went out to fill the kettle, I thought back to the amazing coincidence that happened several years ago now, when I had come to Russets Road on a hospital chaplaincy placement as part of my ministerial training.

It was the first time Ruth and I had met, and I sat where I was sitting now, politely asking and answering questions, until suddenly, a knock came at the door, and a man's grey head appeared around it.

'Oh, sorry, my lover,' he said hurriedly to Ruth. 'I didn't know you was busy.'

'It's all right, Oliver.' Getting to her feet, Ruth had ushered the man, who was tall and distinguished looking, inside. 'This is Carol. She's training to be a minister, and she's going to come here for a few months.'

'Allus glad to meet a minister in training! Anybody who loves the Lord is a friend o' mine, my luv.' My hand was grasped in a firm clasp before a lapel badge was displayed to me. 'I'm a chaplaincy visitor, see. I come in every day now I'm retired.'

'Great.' I nodded, a bit overwhelmed, as I guessed everyone must be, on first meeting his zeal. Then, as he left the chapel, eager to be on his way round the wards, I heard Ruth say: 'Oliver's a Pentecostalist.' And I knew.

To her complete astonishment, I dropped my bag on the floor, got to my feet and ran after the retreating elderly figure.

I caught him up just as he reached the lift. 'You're Oliver Paskin, aren't you?' I panted, looking up and seeing the face I could suddenly recognise from all those years ago. 'You ran the Sunday School at Great Bridgley. I used to be Carol Bentley. I don't suppose you remember . . .'

Oliver scratched his head as he looked wonderingly down at me. 'Yo'm one of them babbies!' he exclaimed. 'Well, I'll be . . . And now yo'm gonna be a minister? Well, praise the Lord!'

Now, it no longer mattered that I had left the Great Bridgley fellowship at the age of thirteen, disillusioned and sceptical. All that mattered was that, against all the odds, God had brought Oliver Paskin back into my life after an absence of thirty years, to share in my joy at being able to follow his example and preach the gospel.

'Penny for your thoughts?' Ruth asked, as she came back to plug in the kettle.

I grinned. 'Just thinking how great it was,' I explained, 'the way Oliver Paskin just *had* to be there to see it, when I was ordained!'

CHAPTER ELEVEN

'I've been waitin' fer yo! I got summat private to say!' Gladys Eliot's monumental tones reached me the moment I walked into the ward.

I hurried to her bedside, where she was seated on her chair dressed in hospital stretch stockings and a royal blue housecoat. A zimmer frame stood incongruously in front of her strong looking figure.

'Draw the curtains!' she bawled. 'They've got ears like Dumbo in this ward!'

'Is that better, Gladys?' I drew the curtains, at the same time giving a consoling smile in the direction of Gladys' two new ward mates. They both steadfastly avoided my gaze. 'Now,' I sat on the bed. 'What is it? Isn't the treatment going well after your operation?'

Gladys glared at me through gimlet eyes. Her brow was creased into lines of anxiety I'd never seen before. 'Nothing wrong with the treatment, apart from the pig swill they feed me, and the time yo has to wait to be took to the toilet!' she said, with familiar bluntness. 'Sides, I'm expecting to go home next wick! No, what I want to say ay really about me at all. It's me lad, Garry.'

'Oh?' I stared in surprise. 'I didn't know you had a son, Gladys.'

Gladys sighed and spread her large, pint pulling hands. 'On'y had the one, nearly tore me insides out having him,' she said. 'He's married, see, or rather, 'e was!'

She went on to explain in a voice lower than I'd have thought her capable of that Garry had been to see her that afternoon and told her regretfully that his marriage was over. His wife was seeing somebody else and he had no alternative but to leave their Gernam Park home and go back to his mother.

'He day want to worry me, specially with me being laid up in here,' Gladys went on defensively, 'but he's got nowhere else to go, and I cor condemn him just cuz he married the wrong wench, now can I?'

I shook my head, realising how hard it must be, nevertheless, for Gladys, always so bluntly critical of outsiders, to admit that all was not well within her own family.

'I don't think it's ever up to us to condemn anyone,' I said. 'Remember what Jesus said about casting the first stone? But I know from my own experience that this sort of thing can be pretty devastating.'

'I know. That's why I told yer!' Gladys replied, the strength beginning to come back to her voice. 'Some of the curates we've had, they've bin no more than kids. They don't know if they'm on this earth, or fullers! But yo've bin through the mill yerself, and yo've got a few lines an grey hairs to prove it!'

'Er, thanks, Gladys.' As I drew back the curtains, I was aware that the other two ladies on the ward were now regarding me with scarcely disguised curiosity. 'I'll pop round and see you when you're back home,' I promised hastily. 'P'raps I'll get a chance to talk to Garry myself then.'

'Ar. We'll sort him out between us, sweetheart!' Almost her perky self again, Gladys gave me a wink before turning her attention to the lunch trolley which had just appeared in the ward doorway.

'About time!' she boomed. 'My belly thinks me throat's bin cut!'

Feeling a bit that way myself, I made my way to the next floor, planning to check on Tom Jenkins before I went home to lunch.

To my surprise, the ward sister told me he had gone to take things easy at home. 'A whole tribe of relatives came to collect him this morning,' she said, with a grin. 'I thought they must've come on a coach!'

'Tom does have loads of children and grandchildren,' I verified. 'I expect Daisy made sure they took him off in style, wrapped up to the ears in woollies!'

'She did better than that!' Reaching under the counter, the sister produced a bright orange carrier bag.

'Hats!' she explained, as I stared in astonishment. 'She knitted them on her machine, in every colour of the rainbow, one for every nurse who so much as gave her Tommy a cup of tea since he came here! I didn't have the heart to tell her most of them wouldn't be seen dead in a woolly hat!'

It depended a lot on the type of woolly hat, I thought, with all the wisdom of a new stepmother, as I later went on my way. Our Edmund wore a woolly hat most of the time.

Making up my mind to visit Tom and Daisy as soon as he had settled at home, I went back to the manse to find Mark fresh in from a staff meeting.

'Mary Watkins rang in her church warden capacity,' he said. 'Apparently, Geoff saw her at the Mothers' Union meeting today and told her about your experience at the early service yesterday.'

'What did she say?' I paused in opening the bread bin. Mary, at sixty, had been involved with St Benedict's all her life, through her mother and grandmother. The first ever female churchwarden there, she had, I knew, been instrumental in my appointment, standing alongside Geoff when he initially persuaded the Parochial Church Council that St Benedict's needed a woman minister.

'What d'you think?' Taking the loaf out of my hand, Mark pulled me close. 'She's with you all the way, of course!' he said. 'She just thought you might like to know that!'

'That's really sweet.' As we sat down to lunch, I thought of the other gestures of warmth and kindness I'd been a witness to, just in that one morning; from Gladys Eliot's grudging respect and request for help, to Daisy Jenkins gratefully extravagant homemade gifts to a bunch of young nurses.

God showed his love in so many strange and wonderful, ordinary and practical ways. In as many different ways in fact as there were people. I only hoped I too could show that love, in a way that would be most helpful, to Dawn and Wayne Mason this afternoon.

As I later set off for Shakespeare Grove, I was again glad that the day was bright and clear. On my way, I had to pass St Benedict's primary school. The noise of young voices told me that the afternoon playtime was in session, and hearing several calls of 'Hello, Mrs 'Afforne!' I stopped and waved, calling out to them in reply.

In a village like Netherley Bank, there was strong continuity, and I guessed that both Dawn and Wayne had come to the local school. It would have been part of their plans, the natural scheme of things, for them to assume that little Simon would eventually come here, too.

'Hello, Reverend.' The barking of the collie heralded my approach at the council flat, and soon Wayne was letting me in. Dawn sat as before on the sofa, her long hair tied back. A blonde woman I vaguely recognised was just getting ready to leave.

'This is my mom,' Dawn said. 'You probably remember her from the other day.'

'Yes.' I took the woman's hand. 'I did see you there.'

Dawn's mother looked straight at me, and as on the day of the funeral, I felt the spark of recognition, of similar background and experience, between us. 'It was a lovely service you did,' she said. 'I wanted to tell you that. Now, like I've been telling these two, we've all got to learn to take one day at a time, and be grateful for what we've got left.'

After she'd gone, I gave Wayne and Dawn the leaflets from the hospital and assured them of Revd Ruth's support.

'That's great of you both, Reverend,' the young man said, as he sat by his wife and put his arm around her, 'but like Dawn's mom says, we're still learning, and some days is worse than others, especially for Dawn. I think we'll pass on the counselling, but we might like to come to a service, if—if the babbies name's mentioned, like.'

'I'm sure it will be, Wayne,' I said. 'And don't forget, we'll be having our special mourners service at St Benedict's next Sunday. Simon will definitely be remembered in our prayers then.'

Dawn and Wayne said nothing, almost embarrassingly drawing apart, she to pat the dog, he to go and make a cup of tea. But before I left 32 Shakespeare Grove, I noticed there was a new photograph of a happily smiling Simon on the wall unit. And standing beside it was his baptismal candle, the one we'd used last time for prayer—now several inches shorter.

I told Mark all about it as we sat quietly in the front room after tea, preparing to say Evening Prayer. It was a beautiful late summer evening, the sun setting over Barlow Hill and the traffic on the road outside beginning to thin.

'P'raps they'll be blessed with another child before too long,' Mark said, thoughtfully. He turned over his page in the Alternative Service Book: 'O God, make speed to save us.'

At that moment, from the bedroom above our heads there came the deafening blast of Edmund's music, shattering the peace into a million fragments.

We exchanged a smile of mingled content and resignation: 'O Lord, make haste to help us!' I replied, fervently.

CHAPTER TWELVE

'Did you get the holy water?' Marcie Danks asked hopefully, the minute I walked through her front door.

'Erm, yes.' Doubtfully, I took out the highly suspect bottle and handed it to her. 'Phyllis Evans brought it back from the Jordan,' I explained, as Marcie frowned at the brackish liquid. 'Geoff says put some salt in it.'

Marcie's eager blue eyes opened wide. 'Oh, why's that?' she asked, stopping dead in her tracks.

Wishing I could supply the mystical answer she obviously expected, I said I was just repeating what Geoff had said. While Marcie bore her prize off to the kitchen to find the salt cellar, I went into the living room to greet my small home communion congregation.

They were all gathered as usual around sweet faced, patient Des, Marcie's once dynamic husband, a man whose quiet spirituality in the face of a great handicap always made me feel both humble and privileged.

'Hi, Des,' I said, giving him a hug, and he grinned.

'Lo, Carol,' he managed to say.

'It always does him good to see you,' Nan, Marcie's middle-aged next door neighbour said from the sofa. 'In fact, that goes for all on we!'

Her companions, an elderly couple who also lived nearby, nodded vigorously. As I set out the communion on the waiting coffee table, and slowly put my surplice and white embroidered stole on over my cassock, I could hear them behind me:

'Don't she look lovely, Nan?'

'Beautiful, Beattie! It does my soul good to come to these little services!'

'Specially now 'er's been done a priest!' the old man put in meaningfully. 'That makes it even better!'

I was glad my back was turned because the unexpected litany of praise was making my face feel like it was turning beetroot colour! Thinking of how different it all was to the rejection I'd felt the day before at St Benedict's, I realised God was really going to town if he wanted to remind me there were still plenty of places where my priesthood was appreciated. He was also doing it with his usual sense of humour!

But there was much more entertainment to come, for suddenly, Marcie appeared from the kitchen, holding the opened bottle of holy water. 'I've put the salt in, Carol,' she said, excitedly. 'I don't know what it's done!'

One thing it definitely hadn't done was kill the smell! Like bad eggs, it rose from the offending vessel. It was, quite simply, indescribable, like all the old-fashioned smelling salts and worst smelling joke perfumes in the world put together.

'Marcie,' I began, with a sympathetic look at poor Des, who was obviously stunned into silence. 'I really don't think you should put this on your husband!'

'No!' Marcie shook her head. 'No! I wouldn't dream on it! Not tonight, with you here. He's never had holy water from a priest before!'

'Well, I . . .' Stepping back, I eyed the vile concoction warily. Then I looked again at Marcie's pleading face, and Des's suddenly encouraging smile. If it really helped, I had to do it.

'Lord.' Gingerly, I put a tip of my finger into the bottle. 'I ask you to bless Des, and as this water touches him,' I tried not to shudder as I wiped the drops down Des's waiting brow, 'may your Holy Spirit cleanse and revive him, bless and keep him and fill him with your peace and joy.'

My task completed, I breathed a sigh of relief and prepared to jam the stopper back in the bottle. Then it came, the chorus of voices from the hearth rug:

'Anoint me, too, Carol!'

'An' me an' Bert!'

'Ooo, just like an *angel*, ay 'er?'

Humbled and bemused, and still marvelling at God's wonderful sense of timing, I passed along the row of suddenly kneeling figures. I couldn't quite believe it was happening, and all I prayed as I dipped my finger again and again into the foul brew was that none of them asked to anoint me in return!

Next morning, just as I was regaling Mark with the story, the telephone rang.

'It's me, Carol,' Marcie Danks said apologetically in my ear. 'About that holy water. It seemed a bit strong when I came to anoint my Des this morning, so I had a bit of a prayer, and the Lord told me what to do.'

'Yes, Marcie.' I held my breath, hoping against hope the Lord had given her good advice.

'Ar,' Marcie went on. 'He told me my Des should have it all in one go, when I washed him.'

'Oh no!' I had visions of poor Des having the bottle emptied over his long-suffering head.

'So I got a bowl,' Marcie went on, while I mentally crossed myself. 'One I was never going to use again, and I poured it all in and made my Des paddle in it! Well, I said, it's from the river Jordan, and that's where our Lord paddled, aye it?'

'From the way you describe the smell, it's probably the same water he paddled in!' Mark said, knowingly, when I went back to finish the story. I had to agree!

It was good to be lighthearted, because the

day was one of meetings. Already I'd had the usual staff meeting following Morning Prayer with Geoff, and later this morning we were off to St Michael's, Gernam Park, for the deanery chapter.

Most of the brothers were assembled when Geoff and I arrived. They sat around a little back room that smelt of musty hymn books and rising damp, precariously balancing cuppa soups over their neatly clerical filofaxes.

'Welcome to the Ritz,' Revd Les Dennis, St Michael's bespectacled incumbent, smiled apologetically. 'Grab yourselves an oxtail or tomato and make yourselves comfortable.'

Mervyn Mitchell, as rural dean, presided at the meeting as usual, reading the notices and introducing the topics. Without Father Brian, the atmosphere was not openly antagonistic, but I couldn't help but be aware of my minority status as the only woman.

'It's how you'd feel if you'd somehow wandered into the changing rooms at the local rugger club,' I remembered describing the feeling to St Benedict's Mother's Union one night. 'As if they can't exactly work out what you're doing there!'

'Wake up, Reverend!' As Mervyn finished talking, Geoff pushed a piece of paper under my nose. 'It's the rota that's gone into the local paper for Merrily Mall,' he explained urgently. 'Look, we're down for October 9th, to do drama!'

'Drama!' I looked around but there was no sign of Revd Derrick Jones. 'We never offered that!'

'No!' came the plaintive voice of part retired minister Clement Dale from the row behind. 'And St Mary's never offered liturgical dance, either, but that's what we're down to do!'

On the short distance back to Netherley Bank, Geoff and I discussed the options. They seemed pitifully small. Either we got some of the congregation to read a passage from the dramatised Bible in the arena at the giant shopping centre, or we trained the Encounter children to act in a proper play.

'Funny Encounter should be this very afternoon, Carol,' Geoff said meaningfully before he dropped me off at the manse. 'I reckon you should go along and see what you can do!'

Muttering to myself, I made my way upstairs to my tiny study. Chapter meetings always left me feeling flat and dispirited, but this was worse than ever. Thanks to someone else's incompetence, I had to sort out some suitable material and cajole a bunch of probably unwilling youngsters to stand up and proclaim the Gospel to a few hundred passing Sunday shoppers!

CHAPTER THIRTEEN

'Miss? Miss?' As soon as I mentioned going to Merrily Mall on a Sunday afternoon, Michelle Jacques' arm had started shooting into the air.

'Just a minute, Michelle.' I looked around the fidgeting circle in the battered parish centre chairs and caught the encouraging eye of Sally, the church warden's loyal daughter. 'I do have a mime here, called "The Sheep Thief"' I explained patiently, raising my voice as they began to talk among themselves. 'Now push your chairs back and we'll have a go before confirmation class.'

As I'd half expected, the only member of Encounter even remotely interested was Katie, Geoff's ten-year-old daughter. Giving her the part of the narrator, I busied myself trying to persuade the others to take parts.

'Zoe, you're only little. You can be the sheep!'

Red-haired Zoe pouted. 'Don't *wanna* be a sheep, miss!'

On cue, the boys, standing as usual on the edge of the group, began a chorus of bleating. 'Will you lot shut up?' Giving Berkley, the loudest sheep of all, a warning look, I turned back to the now mutinous Zoe. 'It's only a little part, Zoe, and it's ever so funny!

'Now, I want another volunteer!' With a

flourish, I pulled a bright red lipstick from my cassock pocket and was nearly killed in the rush.

'Can I wear the lipstick, miss?'

'Me, miss!'

'No, me. I like that colour!'

As another cry of 'Miss, miss!' came from Michelle Jacques, I quickly chose an upturned hand. 'You, Claire. I want you, when Katie reads the word "branded" to go over to Stuart and Christopher, who are the sheep thieves, and write the letters S T in this bright red lipstick on their foreheads!'

'Lipstick or not, I don't think you're going to get this lot into street theatre—not without a lot of bribery and corruption!' Sally said, meaningfully, as we watched the enthusiastic Claire, lipstick in hand, begin to chase the two roaring, galloping boys around the noisy hall.

'I'm beginning to think you're right,' I sighed, clapping my hands. 'All right! I know you're not keen, but we'll just go through it once!'

'Miss! Miss!' Michelle Jacques finally got my undivided attention as the little group of confirmation candidates trailed across to the quiet corner of the stage.

'Yes, Michelle!' I stared down into her blue eyes, thinking as always how angelic she looked. A picture in blue when she took the leading female role in last Christmas's nativity tableau. Maybe, I thought, in a sudden burst of enthusiastic hope, she was going to ask if she could play a major part in Encounter's rendition of 'The Sheep Thief'. If anyone could get the attention of the busily scurrying audience, it was her.

'Please, miss,' Michelle took a deep breath, her face at last able to register her mingled excitement and greed. 'Can we go shopping while we're at Merrily Mall?'

On the way home, I thought long and hard about the youngsters and their quite understandable lack of incentive about the Sunday service venture. Instinctively, I thought back to my own childhood at Oliver Paskin's Pentecostal mission. And the answer came in a flash.

As soon as I got into my study, I rang Mary Watkins. 'Tell me,' I asked, 'is there any money available to take the Encounter kids on an outing?'

Mary's rich laugh bubbled down the line. 'From the look of our Sally when she gets home it's the leaders who need an outing!' she replied. 'But yes, you'll have to check with the church treasurer, but I'm pretty certain a small fund was set aside for that use when the group was started, and no-one's ever asked for it.'

'My plan,' I told Mark, over tea, as Berkley gave an enthusiastic shout of 'Yes!' at my side, 'is to take Encounter on a free trip to Alton Towers! The—er—week after we do our drama at Merrily Mall!'

That evening was our monthly prayer group, made up equally of Anglicans from St Benedict's and Methodists from Mark's chapel.

I sat with Mark in the modern High Street chapel where we were married, waiting for the members of the group to start arriving. The late sunlight poured through the plain windows, so different to the ornate stained glass of my own church.

On the wall behind the polished, flower-laden communion table was an unadorned cross, and above it, a text: 'Trust and Obey.'

Beneath that text, Mark and I had danced on our wedding day, while our joyful, mingled congregations had clapped and sung with all their hearts: 'O happy day, that fix'd my choice, on thee, my Saviour and my God.'

Tonight, members of the same congregations would be mingling again, to share the short act of worship that we alternated at church and chapel.

'Hi, Betty. George!'

'Come in, Martha. Take a seat!'

Martha, a life-long Methodist, naturally sat next to her chapel friends, while the Anglicans drifting in also made a beeline for familiar faces.

'It's going to be a long time,' I whispered to Mark, as we stood up to give the 'Mission Praise' books out, 'before they become real Anglidists!'

He pulled a mock, reproving face. 'Methocans, if you don't mind!'

It really didn't matter, I thought, my heart lifting as I began to lead our committed congregation in the opening prayer. Whatever labels we wanted to stick on ourselves, God could always see right through them.

CHAPTER FOURTEEN

The great nave of St Benedict's had been packed as usual for the event of the monthly memorial or mourners service. Traditionally, in this part of the Black Country, whole families came into church following a bereavement in order to hear the name of their loved one read out during the prayers. It was the one service in the month when we could be assured of full pews and more than average collections.

Standing near the doors with Geoff, I shook hands with the leaving congregation. I recognised several faces from funerals and pastoral visits.

Among the last to leave were the family of Dawn and Wayne Mason. 'Thank you for the lovely service, Reverend Carol,' the young woman said. 'We specially liked what you said in the sermon about the rock, didn't we, Wayne?'

Her husband nodded as he pushed back his spiky hair, and I was glad I'd followed my instinct to preach on the old hymn 'Rock of Ages'. I knew now why God had put the thought into my head. 'Yes, I never thought before but it's true what you said. When you hit rock bottom, you are standing on rock.'

'And the only way then is up, isn't it?' I gave

them both a hug. 'Let me know if you want to go to the hospital service. We can walk up there together.'

I was still basking in the warm glow of knowing I had said something to help the Masons when the disconsolate voice of Clarke Pettisgrew came at my side:

'Might I have a word?'

'Certainly, Clarke.' Making an extra effort, I smiled at the musical director as we walked away from the remnants of the congregation. 'What can I do for you?'

The response he gave me was an almost indescribable sneer. I realised resignedly that the only thing I would ever be able to do to make Clarke Pettisgrew really happy was to disappear into thin air.

'What you can do for me, Reverend Hathorne,' he said, cultured voice quivering with malice as he avoided looking me in the face, 'is to stop encouraging every Tom, Dick and Harry to ignore the churchyard rules!'

'Churchyard . . .?' I stared at him, at the same time aware that Geoff, seeing the last of the parishioners out, was coming concernedly over. 'I'm sorry, Clarke, but I haven't a clue what you're talking about!'

Drawing himself up to his full height, Clarke gave me a look of absolute loathing. '*Dogs*! That's what I'm talking about!' he burst out, pursing his lips as he awaited Geoff's reaction. 'Dogs being allowed to visit the garden of remembrance, right next to my mother's grave! I saw them only yesterday!'

Suddenly, illuminatingly, I realised he was talking about Bob Grainger and his 'boys'!

'I know we have a notice saying "No dogs in the churchyard",' I said, as I finished telling the silently amused Geoff and tutting Clarke the story of the wedding anniversary burial of ashes, 'but Bill and Ben are Bob Grainger's family and they are very well behaved! Apart from that, Bob has been at the service tonight, presumably leaving the dogs in the car, and he says he's going to come again!'

I broke off, thinking of the thin man's pale face as he went up to light a candle for Ada tonight. Although the lines of loss and loneliness were still etched there, I had seen also the very faintest spark of hope in his pale blue eyes.

'I used to be very involved in the church when I was a lad, Reverend Carol,' he'd confided, as we shook hands. 'Believe it or not, I used to play the organ!'

One glance at Clarke Pettisgrew's face, twitching maliciously beneath his beard, told me that Bob's musical interest would carry no weight with him.

'I don't know what Father Geoff here thinks, but I say we can do without newcomers who ride roughshod over the rest of us!' he declared, meaningfully. 'So I suggest this—this person is told to keep his dogs away, otherwise

I shall have no alternative but to tell him myself!'

Geoff sighed and shook his head. I knew he couldn't really support me and keep the rules as a proper vicar should. But what was really disconcerting was that in that moment, I sensed he wished he was a million miles away from St Benedict's and its petty squabbles.

My one satisfaction, when he finally spoke, was that Clarke didn't get the response he was hoping for, either.

'I think you'd better mention to Bob next time you see him that we do have a "no dogs by law" rule, Carol,' Geoff said. 'If we make him welcome enough in church, that shouldn't put him off. As for you, Clarke, perhaps you'd do well to look at our dwindling electoral roll!'

The incident left me feeling both anxious and dispirited. Mark was at his evening service at Woodsite chapel and the boys at Sarah and Andy's, so I decided to do a detour on the way home and visit Tom and Daisy Jenkins.

The volume of noise that came with the opening of their front door reminded me that it was Sunday, their family visiting day. Nevertheless, Daisy drew me delightedly inside:

'Look 'oo it is! Come in, darlin'—just push by!'

I took a deep breath and squeezed through the Jenkins' narrow hall into the brightly furnished, overheated living room. Looking around rather bemused, I saw every seat and arm on the velour puffed three piece suite was taken. Knees protruded over the deep pile carpet on which sprawled half a dozen pre-teen children, mesmerised by a blaring television set. Every adult lap seemed to hold at least one sleeping baby or placidly chewing toddler. Against one wall, a table was set lavishly for tea.

'Is—is it somebody's birthday?' I asked innocently.

Daisy turned her head knowingly to one side before clasping me to her bosom. 'Naaah, darlin'! It's just Sund'y!' she said, then looking critically at me, 'You look tired. Doin' too much, I reckon! Sit down an' I'll get yer a bit o' tay!'

'Where's Tom?' Squashed on the sofa a few moments later, between Daisy's third daughter and son-in-law, I looked curiously around.

Daisy paused in handing me a china cup with 'Mother' printed on it, and a plate of small cakes and sandwiches. ' 'E's in the verandah 'avin' a nap,' she said, in a stage whisper. 'Ackchewly, darlin', I'm glad yo've come today! 'E's been wantin' ter talk to somebody from church.'

Bringing my goodies with me, I followed her pink, cushioned figure out of the blaring living room, through a yellow vinyl covered kitchen and into a small, glass-sided room, warm and full of plants.

92

There, sitting incongruously in a wheelchair, was the slight, white-haired figure of Tom Jenkins, a vivid purple, green and orange knitted blanket over his knees and a pink silk cravat tied carefully under his chin.

'Hello, Tom!' Putting my cup and plate down, I drew up a chair beside him. 'How're you feeling now?'

As Daisy tiptoed diplomatically away, Tom gave a little shrug. 'So-so, vicar,' he said. 'I'm findin' it ay the bein' bad that's the problem, it's the gerrin' better! I'd like ter come back to church, give you a hand. I miss it like anythin'. But I dow know if I can be much use theer anymore!'

I caught his eye, the question and the longing was so obvious there. The old confidence needing a boost. The assurance that he was still loved and needed in the place of worship where he had given so many years of service.

'You'll always be of use, Tom!' I assured him as I lent over to take his hand and say a prayer. 'In fact, I could do with you at my next mid-week communion, to help train young Michael! He still hasn't got a clue what goes on behind the altar!'

Maybe, I thought, as I later went home, full of tea and jokes and stories, Tom would also be able to give me a hand. To sort out that bloomin' Clarke Pettisgrew!

93

CHAPTER FIFTEEN

I was on my way to visit Gladys Eliot the next evening when I bumped into Gwyneth Armstrong, a retired teacher and local eccentric. Gwyneth was one of the keenest contributors to St Benedict's parish magazine, the editorship of which I had inherited as curate.

'I was just on my way to your house with my copy,' she said, excitedly, holding out an envelope. 'Will you see if it's all right?'

Past experience of Gwyneth's copy made me open the envelope warily. But my eyes still nearly popped out of my head as I read:

'Which Sunday School teacher recently gave herself laryngitis shouting about the Ten Commandments? And who on the church council has just been told that the baby his wife's expecting could well be triplets?'

I shook my head disbelievingly. 'You really should be working for the Sun, you know, Gwyneth,' I said, as I watched the evening sunlight bounce off her studious round spectacles. 'Where do you get all this stuff?'

Gwyneth beamed. 'I knew you'd be proud of me!' she exclaimed. 'I've been a real bloodhound this month!'

'Don't you mean news hound, Gwyneth?' I began. But with a wave of her hand she had gone, turning the corner into Chapel Street, where I knew she visited several old ladies.

As I went on my own way, I bumped into several familiar faces, either from my own or Mark's congregation. Like the old-fashioned, much mourned bobby on the beat, a priest on foot is instantly accessible and I reckoned to conduct as much of my ministry in the streets of Netherley Bank as I did behind the more exclusive altar of St Benedict's.

Gladys' bungalow was in nearby Fellows Road, a neat building with a small garden enclosed by a privet hedge. She was looking eagerly through the window as I went up the path, and was at the front door within seconds, despite her zimmer frame.

'Come out the road, George!' she muttered fiercely.

As she opened the door, the dachshund wagged his tail and bounded at me, rolling over ecstatically to be tickled. 'Come on, George!' I tucked him under my arm and followed Gladys into the living room. 'Well, how are you now, Gladys?'

Gladys pulled a staunch face as she sat with difficulty on the sofa. 'I'm all right, thanks to this lad o' mine! Yo' ay met our Garry yet, 'ave yer?'

I shook my head as a round-faced man in his middle twenties came across the room. He looked, I noticed, really uncomfortable.

'This is Carol, our deaconess,' his mother

said, grandly.

'Er, priest, actually,' I rectified, as Garry and I shook hands. Gladys shrugged. 'Cup o' tay?' she asked, and before I could reply, 'put the kettle on, Garry, that's a good lad!'

As he went out into the kitchen, she said, in a voice loud enough to carry to the house next door. 'Took it really bad, 'e has, that little tart doin' the dirty on 'im! Goo in theer and talk to 'im about it, and George and me'll watch the telly.'

As she propelled me into the kitchen from behind, Garry turned, startled, to look at me. In spite of his polite smile, he looked more embarrassed than ever at being confronted by an older woman in a dog collar. Gladys' idea of pastoral care, I reflected, was certainly different to anything we'd been taught at training college!

Setting out china cups and saucers on a tray, the young man mumbled: 'She has to have it done proper like, me mother. Otherwise, I'll get it in the neck!'

Having 'got it in the neck' or at least 'in the ear' from Gladys on several occasions myself, I fully understood. Leaning against the kitchen cupboard, I asked: 'How's she doing, really, since she got home?'

Garry looked surprised and relieved. As the sound of George barking at the television and Gladys bawling at him to be quiet came from the next room, he grinned:

'Great!' he said. 'Just like yo'd expect really. 'Er's a fighter, me mother! In next to no time, I reckon her'll be off that frame and sortin' them out at that church again!'

'Good, we've missed her!' I said, fervently. 'We can do with all the fighters we can get!'

Garry opened a packet of chocolate digestive biscuits and put them on a plate. 'I don't go to church meself,' he said, all in a rush, 'an' well, I know me mother means well . . .'

'But you can do without my advice,' I said quickly, as our eyes met. 'That's okay, Garry. You know where I am if you ever change your mind.'

When the two of us got back to the living room, and Garry put the tray on the coffee table, Gladys looked up from where she was forcing George to sit between her splayed feet. Her face was a picture.

'Told yer er'd sort yer out, my lad!' she said, nodding approvingly at me. ''Er's like yer mother—bin around and sin a few things!'

'Er, well,' I began, as Garry and I looked at each other again. 'I didn't really do anything, Gladys!'

For the first time since I got there, Garry laughed. It was like the sun coming out after a rain storm. 'She did just the right thing, Mother,' he said. 'Now, if you dow mind, I think I'll give the tay a miss an' nip down to the Fox for a quick pint, as yo've got company.'

'That's me lad! He must be feelin' better if 'e's back on 'is beer!' Gladys boomed proudly as he pulled on his jacket and went to the door. 'All I can say is, thank the Lord 'e's got me to look after—to tek his mind off things!'

CHAPTER SIXTEEN

'Carol? It's me, Brenda Mountback!'

The voice on the answerphone was so full of anxiety I scarcely recognised it. 'Can you come round straight away, please? It's Mom. She's been taken really poorly, and she's asking for you!'

Leaving a message for Mark with the boys, I picked up the keys I had just put down, and, dropping them into my briefcase, hurried out of the manse again.

At nearly ten o'clock at night, the High Street was deserted except for the occasional figure of a man leaving one of the pubs, and the usual cluster of desultory looking youths crossing from the coppice. I reached Eliza Smart's little house in record time, and was soon being let in by a distraught, pale-faced Brenda.

'I've called the doctor,' she whispered as she led me down the familiar hall and up the narrow staircase. 'She didn't want me to, but well, you'll see for yourself how bad she is.'

Eliza was lying in bed in the front bedroom, her slight figure scarcely making a hump in the clothes. 'Hello,' I said, taking her small, cold hand. 'What's all this, then?'

'It's Reverend Carol, Mom!' Brenda said, leaning over, when there was no response.

'You asked me to send for her.'

Eliza opened her eyes. With a faint smile of relief and recognition, she said, weakly, 'I wanted you to come and say a prayer, my wench. My Harold's been standing in that corner all day, waitin'!'

She nodded her white head towards the empty corner of the room that was still decorated and furnished in the style of the 1950's. 'I told 'im,' she went on, matter of factly, 'I won't goo till I'm ready!'

At my side, Brenda gave a frightened gasp. 'Oh where is that doctor?' she exclaimed, running distractedly to the window. 'Do you think I should phone again?'

'Come and sit down, love. If they say he's on his way, I'm sure he must be.' As Brenda sat down beside me on the bed, we all three held hands and I began to pray, asking God to protect and strengthen his servant Eliza, and to put his arms around her and help her feel his peace and love deep in her heart.

The words of the twenty-third psalm came into my mind, and holding one warm and anxious hand and one cold, almost lifeless one, I whispered them into the stillness. Then I took out my oil stock and made the sign of the cross on Eliza's forehead and the backs of her hands. Her breath had grown shallow and harsh and the tips of her fingers were already unmistakably darkening.

'She's going to sleep,' Brenda murmured

hopefully as the grip on her fingers was suddenly loosened. 'She'll p'raps feel better if she can get some rest. This has come on her so suddenly.'

'That's how it is, sometimes,' I whispered in reply. The light was so ordinary, the room so plain and unadorned. Yet I knew we were in the presence of death, and also, surrounding and supporting us, the presence of God the Holy Spirit.

As Brenda and I looked at each other over the small elderly figure who in different ways was so dear to both of us, it was as if all time were momentarily suspended. Then came a change in Eliza's breathing, a rattle in her throat, and a moment later, total stillness. Just as at the moment of birth there is the knowledge that another being is suddenly, miraculously present, so both Brenda and I knew. Eliza had gone.

'Lord, now lettest thou thy servant depart in peace,' the beautiful words of the Nunc Dimittis came to me as I stood up and put my hand on the old woman's still warm forehead. 'For—for mine eyes have seen thy salvation.'

'Oh Carol, thank God you were here!' Brenda whispered through the hands which had been covering her face. She trembled and I put my arms around her, wanting to give her the support she so badly needed. But also aware of the dawning shock and sadness within myself.

'I—I can't believe it!' she went on, as we both looked down at the strangely motionless figure. 'Only last week she was talking about baking for Christmas!' she broke off, looking at her watch. 'I—I'd better go round home, let Sam and the kids know,' she said. 'Will you be all right to stay for a few minutes, just in case the doctor . . . ?'

' 'Course,' I nodded and followed her to the front door. 'I'll make some tea while you're away.'

After she had gone, I stood for a little while in the dark back kitchen where Eliza Smart had so recently cut the thorns from her roses for me to carry home. Like Brenda, I couldn't believe she had gone, that never again would she engage me or anyone else with her generous, innovative skills, or her gently broad Black Country humour.

The shock and sadness I had felt earlier threatened to swamp me as I shakily reached for the old metal pot and the bright red tea cosy that had started life as a balaclava helmet.

Sitting at the table, I began to pray, scarcely knowing how to frame the words, aware in any case that words were not really necessary, and God knew that more than anyone.

And then it came, like the most soothing of all possible balm. The memory of the very first time I came to visit here as a new and uncertain deacon.

'Our Brenda said 'er'd asked yer to call, and

I 'ad a stale loaf, so I thought I'll mek the wench some nice bread puddin'!' Eliza explained, puffing a little after climbing, monkey-like, up the back of a chair to get to the top shelf of the pantry.

Brushing aside my offers of help, she'd set the currant and spice-filled Black Country delicacy on the formica topped table. Cutting two big slices, she pushed one in my direction and pulled the other rapturously towards herself.

'With me diabetes, I ay really supposed to eat this,' she confided, through toothless chomps, 'but the way I look at it is this. The longest of my days is short now, and it's no use, when yo'm dead, lying there, thinkin' "I wish I'd had another piece of bread puddin"!'

By the time the doorbell rang, heralding not only the doctor, but Mark, come to see what had happened, I was laughing and crying. Both at the same time.

CHAPTER SEVENTEEN

Geoff came to see me the week after Eliza's funeral. I could tell as soon as I opened the front door that he had come to say something important. The moment of truth had arrived.

'I might as well come straight out with it, Carol,' my colleague said, perching uncomfortably on the edge of the rocking chair. 'I've been offered another job and I've decided, after a lot of prayer, and discussion with Jane, to take it.'

The relief I felt had all to do with the fact that my suspicious warning bells had been right on target. Geoff and I worked well together, and I would be sorry to see him go.

'I can't say I'm really surprised,' I said, as I watched him begin to relax, obviously glad it was out in the open at last, 'but I didn't realise you were looking for a change. I mean, you never said.'

'Well,' Geoff smiled apologetically, 'seven years is a long time and I've been feeling for a while that I've achieved all I can here.'

He broke off, looking through the window at the traffic laden High Street and beyond it to the hillside church and vicarage.

'To tell you the truth, the new job came up nine months ago, before you were priested,' he admitted, 'but I didn't apply, telling myself that with all the flack that might be coming your way, I was more needed here. But then, a few weeks ago, it came up again, with Bishop Paul's recommendation that I should apply.'

'Where is it?' I asked, 'Somewhere in the diocese obviously, if Bishop Paul's involved.'

Geoff could hardly conceal his excitement as he replied, 'It's at Tatchingham Grove, a team rectorship.'

I looked suitably impressed. Tatchingham Grove was a commuter suburb of Wolverhampton, a rather posh area where, coincidentally, Geoff's two girls already went to a private clergy school.

'Jane must be pleased,' I said, 'though we'll miss Katie and Emma, especially at Encounter. When do you actually start?'

Geoff, getting more relieved by the minute that the news was out, took out his diary. 'If all goes according to plan, my last Sunday here should be October 2nd,' he said. 'That should give us chance to get things organised for the interregnum. I'm going to see the wardens this afternoon.'

After he left, I sat for a long time in the quiet front room, trying to gather my thoughts. An interregnum, a time between incumbents, usually lasted, I knew, for anything up to nine months. One of my colleagues on post ordination training had just gone through one, and I knew how much it had taken out of her, in spite of the support of the church wardens.

If Geoff was leaving, our church wardens, Mary and the lesser involved Trevor Phipps, would be called upon to play a much more active part in the running of the church and we had the added complication of no longer having an active verger.

'Lord,' I prayed silently, 'what are you doing?'

Thinking of the two congregations which already existed at St Benedict's, the schism Geoff had feared because of those who could not accept my sacramental ministry, I could see we were heading for deep water!

In the meantime, though, we had to behave as if nothing were happening, because traditionally, the announcement of Geoff's new post must not become common knowledge until announced in both churches—the one he was leaving and the one he was going to—on a date decided by the bishop and agreed on by both sets of church wardens.

Already it was getting complicated, and I tried to forget about it as I prepared for my next appointment, a funeral visit in Drake Street.

Walking down the High Street, I bumped into Stella, with Antonia in her pushchair. The young woman chatted about her forthcoming wedding and the little girl's growing excitement about taking part in the ceremony.

'Keith says he doesn't believe in God, you know,' she said, thoughtfully as we stopped outside the post office, 'but he always says "thank God!" when something goes right, and he knows how much it means to me, being married in church. He's really lovely. I don't know what 'Tonia and I would do without him!'

Those words echoed in my thoughts as I was later shown into the living room of Mrs Jenny Davidson's house in Drake Street.

Although the whole house was obviously someone's pride and joy, furnished with a comfort verging on the luxurious, the atmosphere was of absolute, abject desolation.

The Davidson's two big, grown-up sons were there, filling the tasteful room with the rawness of their sudden bereavement while their two young wives hovered around their mother-in-law, solicitous and almost guilty in their grief.

Jenny Davidson just sat there, a handsome woman of fifty in a designer track suit. Over and over again she shook her head of thick, raven black hair as she was forced, by my sudden presence, to retell the nightmare of the day before.

'Tony went off to work on the afternoon shift as usual, kissed me by the front door, like he always does. And I got on with the ironing before I got ready for my own work.'

I already knew from Turleys that Tony Davidson, aged fifty-one, had suffered a massive heart attack at work and died before the ambulance could get there.

'Why?' Jenny went on, as I sat down and took the cup of stewed tea one of the daughters-in-law mechanically handed me. 'That's all I keep asking myself. Why? What had my Tony ever done to deserve to die like that?'

I reached out to touch her hand, but there was no response, and her skin felt cold and lifeless. I sighed. 'It's not a question of Tony doing anything,' I said, uncomfortably aware that they were all looking at me almost as if they expected me to produce a magic wand. 'He was obviously very ill, and . . .'

'That's our little grandson, Jamie.' Jenny nodded brokenly to a framed photograph on top of the television set. 'He's five. Tony always called him his little pal. We don't know what to say to him!'

I swallowed, the waves of anger and resentment almost tangible. I knew exactly how it felt, because at the time my own father died, coincidentally from a heart attack at fifty-one, I had been an unbeliever, too.

'I—I don't know either,' I admitted, 'except to tell him the truth, that his grandad loved him, and—and love goes on.'

I thought about the children of St Benedict's, and their unanswerable questions, questions that were all a part of the faith and sense of wonder that seemed to come naturally to them.

'If—if Jamie goes to Sunday School . . .' I went on, hopefully.

'He doesn't.' The taller of the two sons stepped in front of me, blocking my vision of his now sobbing mother. As he almost snatched the empty cup from me, I felt the anger and despair in the beautiful room expand even further, like a balloon filled with black fog.

'Our Dad always said it was a great big fairy story!' my verbal assailant went on, his tear-ravaged eyes like stones as they held mine in an unflinching fierce gaze. 'And after what's happened to him, we know he was right!'

Feeling very sad, I left the Davidsons to their terrible loss and pain. As I made my way home, I felt bruised inside, seeing things because of my own experience, their way. Knowing only too well that to them the church must seem like a lot of salesmen trying to sell them something that was worse than useless, because it didn't satisfy their need in life, which was to simply go on forever, in the love and comfort of their family.

I knew from many other similar funerals I had done that Tony Davidson's last journey to Netherley Bank crem would be accompanied by dozens of floral tributes and many, many followers. That because of his age and popularity, extra chairs would have to be set out in the chapel, and the car park would be choked with traffic.

But there would be no peace in the hearts of his bereft family, only the agony of feeling broken and cheated. As if the God they said they didn't believe in had materialised, merely to smite them with a sledge hammer in the place where it would hurt the most.

By the time I reached the manse I was feeling well and truly depressed, my mind struggling with all the events of that day, starting with Geoff's decision to leave the parish.

'Cazza?' began Berkley immediately I walked through the back door. 'D'you think Dad'll let me have a drum kit?'

I took one look around, at the untidy kitchen, at his school bag and blazer lying discarded in the middle of the hall floor, the dogs waiting to be fed and walked, and something just snapped inside me.

'Why not?' I yelled, dragging off my dog collar and stomping childishly past, up the stairs towards the haven of my study. 'Let's go the whole hog and have a bloody brass band!'

'Pardon?' Openmouthed, Mark's head appeared from the direction of our bedroom, where he had been changing after a ladies' meeting. I took one look at his concerned yet calm face and burst into tears!

'It's Geoff! He's leaving!' I wailed, as he put his arms around me. 'And I've been on a funeral visit, and I feel so sorry for the family! There—there's just no comfort I can offer them!'

Sitting on the bed beside him, I described the scenario in the Davidsons' home. 'I suppose it's worse, knowing how they feel,' I finished, drying my eyes. 'At my father's funeral, I hated the minister. I wanted to tell him to stop insulting us with all his talk about "sure and certain hope"!'

'Then you do have something to offer them,' Mark said. 'God will use that experience to help you conduct that service with a sensitivity that somebody else might not have! And apart from that, think of the other sort of funeral we have, where it's a celebration because people do believe!'

He was right, I realised as the slam of the back door told me Edmund was home. As I went into the bathroom to wash my face, I thought of Eliza Smart's funeral.

Held in church, with all the members of the Mothers' Union present, it had, in spite of the family's sorrow, been a very joyful occasion. The choir, led from the front row of mourners by Brenda's beautiful, brave contralto voice, had sung an anthem, 'God be with you till we meet again.' And I had felt very strongly that Eliza, deliciously full with all the heavenly bread pudding she could eat, was singing it with us.

Afterwards, we had processed out to 'Thine be the Glory!' and the atmosphere had been charged with all the love and support of our church family.

'Anyway,' Mark said, a moment later, meeting me on the landing in his jeans and tee shirt. 'Tell me more about Geoff!'

'I will,' I promised, going back to find my own more comfortable clothes. 'I'll tell you everything while we're walking the dogs.'

As we went outside a few minutes later, a grubby, disconsolate figure glowered up at me from cleaning his bike.

'Sorry, Berkley,' I said quickly, reaching down to ruffle his springy curls.

'S'okay, Caz, it's prob'ly the manypause,' he said. And then, as the sound of Edmund's rap music thundered from within, competing with the excited, pre-walk barking of the dogs, 'Hey Dad. I just asked Cazza. C'n I have a drum kit?'

CHAPTER EIGHTEEN

'Now mek sure yo' wash the vicar's hands, lad,' Tom Jenkins told Michael, from his wheelchair in the chancel. 'This much wine, an' this much werter. Pass me that cruet, would yer, vicar?'

Obediently, I put the old glass jug into the gnarled hands. 'Now yo' put the lavarby towel over yer left arm, see?' As Tom demonstrated self importantly, I escaped into the vestry to change out of my robes.

My thoughts went back to Geoff's announcement, which I was discussing with the church wardens on Monday. How I was going to cope alone with the pastoral care of the 12,000 souls in the parish, I still didn't know. But I was able to send up a silent prayer of thanksgiving that Tom was back, albeit in a training capacity, and that before long, Gladys Eliot's strident tones would also be heard in St Benedict's again, helping to take care of the practicalities.

To add to the regulars, there was also Bob Grainger who, even after being quietly told he couldn't bring his 'boys' to Ada's grave, still continued to come to church.

'I'd forgotten how comforting it is,' he'd said only last week, when I sat at his table for coffee after the service. 'And the music's great!

I tried to tell your organist, but well, he is a funny chap, isn't he?'

I knew I also had support from within the wider community of Netherley Bank, where I found I was being increasingly requested to do funerals for non-churchgoing families, even when as in the case of Tony Davidson, I felt I could offer very little comfort. Baptisms by 'the lady vicar' were also another regular request.

My main concern was what would happen to the anti-woman-priest element in the congregation, once there was no male president available here at St Benedict's.

'Let them leave!' had been Mark's straightforward reaction when we sat up late discussing it. Pulling me close, he'd reminded me, 'Remember that article the bishop had you all read on your ordination retreat, all about "gut lag"? Well, some of these people are obviously suffering from that. They thought they could accept a woman behind the altar, but when they actually saw one, breaking the bread, saying the words of consecration, they found they couldn't take it!'

'So I'm never going to convince them I've been called by God. Is that what you're saying?'

Mark had sighed. 'Maybe some of them, if they let their gut reaction catch up with their brains and hearts,' he replied. 'I just don't know, darling. What I do know is this

114

interregnum could well be the way God is sorting things out at St Benedict's, separating the sheep from the goats, so to speak. So, as I say, let them leave. I'm just relieved none of 'em are likely to become Methodists!'

'Er, excuse me, Carol. Could I have a word?' I turned, startled, as a knock came at the open vestry door.

A vaguely familiar woman of about my own age stood looking anxiously at me. 'I'm Helen Jacques,' she began as I ushered her inside. 'I've come to take my turn with the flowers, but I wanted to see you about our Michelle, and this outing.'

'Oh yes,' I smiled, remembering the keen response of the Encounter members to the news that a trip to Alton Towers was on offer. 'I'm afraid it's something of a bribe, Helen,' I explained. 'As Michelle's probably told you, we want the youth group to take part in a Sunday service at Merrily Mall, doing some drama.'

The other woman sighed and shook her shaggily permed fair head. 'Yes, I heard you preach about it the other week,' she said. 'The thing is, Carol, I've told our Michelle she's grounded! There'll be no outing for her, the way things are going on!'

As we sat on a vestry bench, she explained worriedly that Michelle had been staying out past her nine o'clock deadline and hanging around in the coppice with some rough-looking older girls and boys.

'I've heard there's glue sniffing and allsorts going on over there at night, Carol,' she went on anxiously. 'And I know a gang of them goes around vandalising the place!'

'I know,' I sighed, thinking of the ever increasing problems in the area. 'The trouble is, we've just got another lot of kids who've left Netherley Bank High School with no qualifications and no work to go to!'

'Michelle's dad's worried stiff, cos she's always on about lads, and 'er's such a bonny looking kid,' Mrs Jacques sighed, and shook her head, 'but 'er's mentioned you lots of times, and the things you do at the parish centre. 'Er cried her eyes out when I said 'er couldn't go on the outing with the others.'

'Then p'raps you should let her go,' I suggested thoughtfully, 'but on consideration that she keeps to her deadline in future and tells you where she's going, and who with. And I'll keep my eye on her in Sunday School and at Encounter, and make sure she comes straight home.'

Memories of when Sarah was young flooded back as I watched Michelle's mum go into the nave to begin her work on the flowers. We'd had to have rules too, but they had paid off in the end.

Later, as Michael pushed the still animated Tom home in his wheelchair, I crossed the road to the manse. To my surprise, I found a bright blue pushchair parked outside and

116

inside, shouts of glee echoed amid the barking of the dogs.

'Tonia's having a great time with your little boy!' Stella Tonks called from the front room, as I caught a glimpse of Berkley being happily chased into the kitchen by the ecstatic tot. 'Your husband said I should come in and wait for you.'

'I'm glad you've come, Stella,' I said. 'I was going to contact you this weekend about the wedding rehearsal.'

Stella's pretty face creased into a smile. 'Yes, I told Keith you would be. You did my friend Kerry's wedding the other week, and she said they had to come for a rehearsal.'

'Okay, let's book it up now then, shall we?' I found my diary and sat down opposite her. 'I expect your friend told you we need the best man, your dad, oh, and the bridesmaid, of course!'

'Steady, Antonia!' Stella nodded happily as the three-year-old, chased by Berkley now, rushed in to bury her head in her lap. 'Honestly, we're all looking forward to it all so much! This wedding's going to be really special!'

As her eyes met mine over the little girl's head, neither of us had any way of knowing just how special—and potentially disastrous—Stella and Keith Tonks wedding ceremony was going to be!

CHAPTER NINETEEN

'Is everything all right, Carol?' asked Ruth as I helped her clear away the extra chairs after the hospital memorial service the following Monday. 'You don't seem like your usual bouncy self!'

I shook my head, wishing I could tell her about Geoff leaving and that night's meeting with him and the church wardens to discuss the coming interregnum.

'Just tired, I think,' I replied, handing her a pile of collected service sheets. 'We seem to be getting an influx of weddings, baptisms and funerals with my name on, and it's ages till our gang takes off for the USA.'

I brightened as I thought of the prospect of the planned holiday, our first as an extended family of six. We were going to fly to New York, then hire a van and drive up the east coast into Maine, visiting Mark's relatives on the way.

Panic suddenly hit me, as I realised that of course, by then, we would be well into our interregnum. Mentally, I put holiday cover down as another item on the agenda for the evening meeting.

'Anyway,' I changed the subject quickly as I realised my colleague was staring curiously at me. 'I thought the service was great! Thanks,

Ruth.'

'Thank you for doing the reading and the prayers,' she smiled as she led the way to her office. 'I thought your Dawn and Wayne especially appreciated being here.'

'Her mum came, too,' I replied, remembering the supportive blonde woman at Dawn's side. 'And she comes from the old tradition that says you don't let professional outsiders interfere in your family life!'

I sat down, looking out across the chapel. It had surprised me just how many people had turned up for the special service commemorating children who had died. As Ruth had told me, there were several couples in their fifties and sixties who had lost children at birth or even before birth many years ago and never been able to properly mourn them. This way, they were at last acknowledged, prayed for by name, and so commended into the care of their heavenly Father.

Feeling in need of a little fresh air and exercise when I got home, I took Becky to the coppice, Gran snoring too loudly to be disturbed in Mark's study.

I had gone a little way towards the children's playground when the figure of Michelle Jacques suddenly appeared out of nowhere. 'Lo, miss,' she said, conversationally, falling into step with me.

'Hello, Michelle. Just come out of school?' I asked.

She nodded. 'Your Berkley's on the bus,' she said. Then, almost shyly, she continued, in a rush. 'Thanks again, miss, for gettin' me mom to let me go to Alton Towers!'

I sighed, wondering not for the first time how I could get over to her that this wasn't an easy option. 'I already told you at Sunday School, Michelle,' I said. 'You've got to follow your mom and dad's rules to prove you're growing up and can be trusted with privileges.'

'I know!' she gave a sigh and we walked in step for a while, the dog dancing ahead of us. As we walked we chatted, about Netherley Bank, about church and school, and the subjects she took in common with Berkley. I found myself laughing aloud at some of her antics and expressions.

'You know, Michelle,' I said, before we parted on the other side of the road. 'I was in a bad mood until I got talking to you. You've really cheered me up!'

'Me, miss?' Michelle blinked her blue eyes, seeming to grow visibly by inches as I nodded. 'See yer on Sunday!' she called, as she disappeared, skipping, towards the corner shop.

In order to keep up the discretion, the church wardens meeting was held at Mary's house at Upper Briersley.

'Come on, love, have a glass of sherry while we're waiting!' our lady church warden greeted me warmly. 'Are you going to stay, Mark?'

'No, thanks, Mary,' my husband shook his head. 'I'm just dropping Carol off,' he explained, giving me a goodbye kiss. 'I'm due at a circuit property meeting at seven thirty!'

'Rather him than me!' Mary chuckled, as I came in from seeing him off. 'Sit down, Carol. Geoff and Trevor shouldn't be long. And tell me about this play you're doing with the kids. From what Sally says it should be fun!'

'It should,' I agreed, and then, as it hit me like a ton of bricks, 'except that the narrator is Katie Hanson, and of course, she'll be in Tatchingham Grove by the time it takes place!'

Geoff arrived just then, followed closely by Trevor Phipps. Trevor was a mild tempered little man who, until his business was taken over the year before, had been quite an affluent member of the congregation. He now worked part time as an adviser to small business entrepreneurs and spent his spare time on church matters.

'Hi, Carol,' he said, giving me a peck on the cheek. 'I see we've driven you to drink already!'

'Do join us,' Mary put two more glasses on the tray. 'It's probably going to be quite a long meeting!'

After we had begun with prayer, Geoff was able to tell us the date the bishop had decided the announcement should be made, at both Netherley Bank and Tatchingham Grove. It was a week on Sunday, after which Geoff and his family would be taking a fortnight's leave.

'I s'pose that's what you call "hit and run"!' Trevor muttered into his sherry.

Geoff stared at him and then looked away again, a dark flush mounting his face. 'Not really, Trevor, the holiday's been planned for months,' he replied.

In the suddenly tense atmosphere, Mary and I exchanged a glance. 'Oh well, not to worry. It'll just give us the chance to find out how we manage on our own, won't it, Carol?' she said.

CHAPTER TWENTY

By the end of August, the news was out that Geoff was leaving. It was greeted, as I had expected, with a mixed reaction.

The days had gone when vicars stayed for twenty-five years, even in a place as settled and traditional as Netherley Bank, and many in the congregation said they weren't surprised that Geoff was moving on, that it was in a sense, time for a change.

My own most stalwart supporters like Marcie Danks and her friends wanted to know straight away if that meant I could be the vicar now. Then I had to explain that I didn't really have the experience to run a parish this size single-handed.

Actually, I was happy as I was for the time being. Even though I knew I would soon have to cope with a lot more work and responsibility, it would, hopefully, not be for that long, and it would be very good experience.

Others in St Benedict's church family were not, I knew, at all pleased with the prospect of being left with a woman priest. The first to leave were the Fishers, who came to see Geoff while I was at the vicarage one day.

'It's not that we have anything against Carol personally,' Norma was at great pains to point

123

out. 'We both like her very much and think she does a great job pastorally around the parish. It's just that we can't accept scripturally that a woman can represent Jesus.'

'And especially speak in church!' Jim, the more vociferous of the two, put in while Norma firmly nodded. 'You know what St Paul says about that!'

Geoff met my eyes consolingly. 'He also said that in Christ, we're all equal—no slave nor free, no Jew nor Gentile, no male nor female!' he reminded them quietly. 'Well, we'll be sorry to lose you both, but if that's how it must be . . . Where are you going, anyway?'

Norma's round face almost burst with enthusiasm. 'Wayback Christian Fellowship in Gernam Green,' she replied. 'You've probably seen their minibus. It comes round the estate on Wednesdays!'

'They do a great job, too,' I heard myself say quietly. 'Picking up the old folks and taking them to fellowship services, running a club for the kids in the school holidays. I wish we were as well organised!'

Though I knew it had to be, I was sad and disappointed that the Fishers finally had to admit that they could not accept my ministry. And I couldn't help but feel guilty, too.

Over the years they had, I knew, devoted their lives to St Benedict's. It was their grandchildren who made up a large proportion of our Sunday School.

Although they had said right away that they would not try to influence their churchgoing sons and daughters into leaving, I wondered gloomily just how long it would be before they joined their parents at the Wayback Fellowship.

The others in church who now made it a practice to only attend Geoff's communion services—boycotting mine—were more difficult to handle. There had, I knew, been a definite shocked reaction to the news that they would soon be without a 'proper' priest, and Geoff was told of hurt feelings and emotions of being betrayed and cheated.

'We thought we'd always be able to rely on you, Father Geoff,' one stalwart communicant said, and was far from pleased by my colleague's response that he was not, to paraphrase Jesus, 'leaving them priestless.'

But it was Clarke Pettisgrew's reaction that I was most wary of, and the day of the announcement, I watched his red face turn several shades more ruddy behind the mask of his beard. When the service was over, he simply got up from the organ, tore off his robes, and slammed out. He banged the vestry door without saying a word to anyone.

'He'll be back,' Geoff predicted, 'he's just narked because he wasn't the first to know!' But we both knew that the angst of our superior director of music went deeper than that, and I couldn't help but feel distinctly uneasy.

The mood continued through my already busy days in the parish, days filled with pastoral visits, funerals and meetings. With the interregnum on the horizon, the meetings were more frequent, and I found myself out most evenings, in discussion with the church wardens and various sub-committees of the Parochial Church Council.

It was the part of parish ministry I least enjoyed and found most tiring, so that by the Saturday of Stella and Keith's wedding, I was feeling less than my best.

Geoff and his family had now gone on holiday, leaving for Cornwall with a more than usual relief and elation. So the church, the choir, and the sulking Maestro were all under my control.

'Welcome to St Benedict's!' I whispered, as Stella came through the great doors on her father's arm. 'You look lovely! And so do you, Antonia!'

The tiny bridesmaid was entrancing in a pale lilac floral dress. She carried a hoop of flowers, and she literally danced down the aisle after her pretty mother.

All through the service, and especially during the hymns, Antonia danced, thoroughly enjoying herself as she whirled across the chancel. From behind the organ, Clarke Pettisgrew glowered—disapproving of everything that was going on, but mostly of

126

me, a woman, daring to bless the young couple, to pronounce them man and wife, and at the end of the service, to extend that blessing to the rest of the huge congregation of their family and friends.

Feeling suddenly very tired, I followed the choir back into the vestry. After the prayer of dismissal, someone put the kettle on and made a cup of tea. And it wasn't until we were all sitting down enjoying it that Brenda Mountback suddenly looked across the table and said thoughtfully: 'Hey, Carol. You know that couple didn't say their vows, don't you?'

'P-pardon?' I stared at her in the sudden silence of the listening choir, as waves of horror went over me, realising in a split second that the service I had just conducted had seemed very short. And why. 'Of course they did!' I said, automatically.

'They didn't, love.' Brenda was lovely and we'd been through a lot together, lately, but in that moment all I wanted was for her to shut up, or to be saying anything but what she was saying. 'I thought it must be because they'd already got a kiddie. I heard you include her in the prayers.'

My heart thudding, I picked up my service book. Too late, I saw exactly what I had done. The order of service went from the bride and groom saying 'I will', through the vows, to the blessing of the rings—and I had turned over two pages instead of one!

'Quick!' Reaching out, I grabbed Michael. 'Run and see if they're still out there having their photographs taken. And if they are, bring them back in!'

So long as there was some congregation, and the vows were said in their hearing, surely, I thought, it would be all right. Embarrassing for me, but that was the price I had to pay for being so careless!

Michael came back a few moments later to say Stella and Keith's car had already left, and the next bridal party was on its way through the lych gate!

'What are you going to do, love?' Brenda asked concernedly, as the choir, talking amongst themselves, went out into the south aisle. 'Will you get into trouble?'

I shook my head, unable to speak as I tried to think things through. Stella and Keith would be on their way to the reception at the Hillman Arms by now. She had excitedly told me all their plans and I knew that after the reception, they were going on honeymoon to Weymouth.

'It's the first time we've been on holiday as a family, Reverend Carol, and the first time Antonia will see the sea!' I could almost see her bright face as she discussed all aspects of this marriage.

Marriage . . . Were they really married, after what I'd done, or rather, hadn't done, in the ceremony? I went through the next wedding so carefully, checking and re-checking, feeling

128

Brenda's sympathetic eyes on me from the choir stalls.

Then, I ran home and almost hysterical by now, told Mark what had happened.

'Now hang on a minute.' He sat me in the rocking chair and squatted in front of me. 'You say they exchanged rings and clearly the intention was for them to get married?'

'Yes, but—but they didn't say the vows!' I exclaimed, wildly. 'Not even a word of them! How could I have been so stupid? After all the weddings I've done!'

'You've not done many as a priest, and you've an awful lot on your mind at the moment,' Mark reminded me. 'Look, I'm pretty sure that legally, they are married. It's what they call irregular, but not illegal.'

'But shouldn't we go to the Hillman, fetch them back?' I gabbled. 'It's not too late.'

'By the time we get over there and back it will be,' Mark reminded me. 'It's nearly five thirty now, and don't forget you can't marry anyone after six pm. That is the law!'

How on earth, I wondered, was I going to cope in an interregnum if I made mistakes like this before Geoff left? And what would he, my colleague, think of me when he got back and found out what I'd done?

St Benedict's, with its magnificent building and gorgeous view was a favourite church for weddings, but people wouldn't want to risk getting married there if they thought I was an incompetent priest.

After a sleepless night, I went to preside at the Sunday morning Eucharist, and found a definite atmosphere.

'Did you find them, love?' Brenda asked me, worriedly. 'Did you manage to put it right?'

I shook my head, trying not to show how anxious I still was. 'No, but Mark's pretty sure it's okay and they are married,' I said.

On Monday, we had decided we would take further advice through the Diocesan legal department. After a morning on the telephone, no one was prepared to tell us anything absolutely specific about the legality of Stella and Keith's marriage, but it was promised that it would be thoroughly investigated.

'There's nothing more we can do now, darling,' Mark reassured me as we went into the front room for special prayers. 'You're just going to have to forget about it until we hear something definite.'

On Wednesday morning, in the post I received a postcard from Weymouth.

'Just to say we're having a great time and to thank you for the beautiful service, especially for the prayers. Antonia loved it when you mentioned her name.'

'How can I, after getting this, turn round and tell them I messed their wedding up?' I asked Mark. 'I—I can't bear to think of them having to go through with it all again!'

'Relax, darling!' Not for the first time, I thanked God for Mark's wonderful support as he took the card and placed it on display on the mantlepiece. 'They still might not have to, if the Diocese does its homework properly!'

For the rest of that week I carried on my ministry in Netherley Bank quietly relieved that it was August, the traditionally quiet time in the church year.

I visited the still unresponsive Davidson family, took communion to all three local nursing homes, and did my usual stint of visiting at Russets Road hospital. But it was still one of the longest weeks of my life, and by the time Saturday came I felt I was really living on my nerves, and needing every moment of my panic-stricken times of fearful and fervent prayer.

Something inside me—another of God's warning bells—was telling me unmistakably that Stella and Keith's missed wedding vows were only the beginning of a nightmare yet to come. So hearing from Geoff the minute he got home from his holiday didn't surprise me one little bit.

'I've just had a phone call from Bishop Paul, Carol,' my colleague said, sounding tired and sympathetic and worried, all at the same time. 'Someone has sent him an anonymous letter about you!'

CHAPTER TWENTY-ONE

'They've certainly not wasted any time,' Geoff sighed, as I finished telling him about Stella and Keith's wedding and the panic of the past week. 'I've asked Bishop Paul to send us a copy of the letter, which purports to come from the whole congregation, but in the meantime, I think we should all pray very hard because I've been feeling for some time that we're under attack here.'

Drawing the curtains against the suddenly bleak evening, Mark lit a candle and the three of us sat silently watching its flame.

My mind was in a turmoil. As I pressed my cold hands together, all I could think was that a group of people in the congregation I had come to love so much had not only put a knife in my back, but thoroughly twisted it.

It was exactly like being hurt and rejected by close family members and I felt I couldn't bear the pain.

'I know I made a mistake,' I whispered, when Geoff and then Mark had offered prayers, asking for God's love and support at this time, 'but we're trying hard to put it right. Stella and Keith are due home from holiday soon, and I've already planned to get in touch with them as soon as I can.'

'The really worrying thing,' Geoff said,

reluctantly, 'and I hate to tell you this, Carol, is that whoever sent the letter is threatening to go to the newspapers!'

'Oh no!' I went hot and cold, feeling trapped and very much afraid. 'Surely it's not much of a story?' I looked for verification from one to the other of my companions and my heart sank as they both shook their heads.

'I suppose it depends what else is around at the time, darling,' Mark said. 'I bet the local papers wouldn't turn their noses up at it!'

That night, I tossed and turned, unable to sleep. I imagined the ridicule not only of myself, but of Stella and Keith who had saved so hard and made such preparations for their wedding. At the memory of that happy postcard, I bit my lip.

'Try not to worry too much, darling,' Mark, awake too, held me close. 'The ones to be pitied are the ones who sent the letter, and I think we've both got a pretty shrewd suspicion about who their ringleader is!'

'It's just the hatred behind it all,' I replied, brokenheartedly. 'The thought that they— he—would go to such lengths to get me into trouble!'

Mark sighed as he smoothed back my hair. 'I bet if you asked three-quarters of ministers they've all done something that's landed them in trouble,' he said. 'The ones that are any good, that is! As Geoff says, we're the ones who come under attack, and the devil doesn't mind what weapons he uses. But we've got the best of all weapons—prayer!'

The letter arrived at the vicarage two days later.

'My Lord,' it said, in refined, spidery handwriting. 'A group of us parishioners at St Benedict's parish church, Netherley Bank, are most concerned about the behaviour of our curate, Rev Carol Hathorne. She is foul-mouthed, flippant and totally irresponsible. Her latest outrage has been to conduct a wedding without vows! In our opinion, in this fiasco, the couple were not married at all! The vicar either does not know or does not care, as he is leaving shortly. Unless something is done immediately, we shall be informing the newspapers about the wedding that never was.' It was signed 'A group of parishioners.'

The next day in church I felt ill and preoccupied. Several of the congregation asked if I was all right, and although my heart told me I could trust their concern, my head told me that they could be part of the plot against me.

Through a mist, I saw that Gladys Eliot was back, aided by sticks, in her usual pew, peering at me suspiciously as I went down to share the peace. 'What's up wi' yo'?' she demanded.

Glad of being spared having to answer, I smiled and turned to take the proffered hand of young Michelle Jacques, making a special effort to greet me as the Sunday School came back in from their lessons. 'Peace, miss.'

Behind the altar, Clarke Pettisgrew seemed his usual arch self, and remembering our suspicions and the tone of the anonymous letter, I wondered if we had been wrong. Surely he would have crowed a little if he had really been able to do me such a damage?

All I could do was hope and pray that the letter writers would not carry out their threat and go to the newspapers.

On the Wednesday morning, just as I was preparing to cross over to say Morning Prayer, the doorbell rang. A young woman, smartly dressed, and in her late twenties, stood there.

'Reverend Hathorne?' she began, as my heart sank. 'I'm Angela Fields from the *Echo*. It's about this wedding you did . . .'

My heart was thumping hard as I led her into the hall. 'You've had a letter, I take it.' I took a deep breath, praying hard. Mark had gone off to a staff meeting, so I was alone in the house.

The girl kept trying to ask me questions, mainly about the young couple, whose name she badly wanted to know. But somehow I fielded the questions, grimly hanging on, repeating time and again that I had nothing to say except that I had made a blunder and it was being sorted out by the church's legal department. Finally, I told her very bluntly to leave.

The next few minutes were a blur of rushing

across to the vicarage, telling Geoff, and deciding what to do.

'I've phoned the Diocese and they say they're preparing a statement,' he said, as he pushed a cup of coffee into my hands. 'Meanwhile, the best thing you can do is go and see your newlyweds and get them back to church—today if possible.'

Knocking on the door of Stella and Keith's flat was one of the hardest things I've ever had to do.

'Reverend Carol!' the young woman exclaimed, as she came out, Antonia at her side. 'I never expected you!'

The little girl, still dancing, took my hand. 'Bucket 'n' spade,' she said. 'Mommy 'n' Dad . . .'

'She hasn't stopped talking about it,' Stella said, as she led me inside. 'We had a marvellous honeymoon, and a beautiful wedding. Thank you.'

'Oh Stella.' I put my hand out to stop her flow of words. 'You won't be so free with your praise when you know why I'm here,' I said, quietly. 'Did you or Keith notice anything about your wedding ceremony?'

Puzzled, Stella shook her head. 'No. It all went by in a flash.'

'Precisely,' I sighed. 'It was shorter than it should've been because I turned over two pages in the marriage service and forgot to get you to say your vows!'

I held my breath then, waiting for the poor

girl to burst into tears or to give me a tirade of abuse. Instead, she shook her head disbelievingly. 'Are you *sure* you missed something out?' she asked, and with a contented smile. 'It all felt very complete to me, and it looks perfect on the video.'

Video! My already plummeting spirits took a further nose dive. I'd forgotten that Stella and Keith's wedding was one of those recorded by a camcorder to be shown to relatives and friends, and, horror of all horrors, to the press? And what about those television programmes, which got their ratings by showing hilarious and horrendous mistakes made at family weddings?

'Anyway,' somehow pulling myself together, I told Stella quickly, 'what we really need is for you and Keith to come back to church—today if you can—and say your vows. Do you mind doing that, Stella? It'll only take a few minutes.'

'Well, if you're sure we need to,' Stella replied, uncertainly. 'Keith's at work but he comes home for lunch. We could get ready quickly and pop round then. About one thirty?'

'I'll be waiting with some witnesses,' I said as I left. As I went back to the manse I silently thanked God for helping me through the ordeal of my confession to Stella. There was something so special about both her and her response to my bombshell that was fast

137

showing this nightmare in a different light.

It was as if the little party of three, Mom, Dad and Antonia, back in their wedding finery and walking down the aisle of St Benedict's that quiet lunch time were suffused by the warmth and power of the Holy Spirit. Met by a hurriedly summoned Mary Watkins and Sally I was given a consoling hug that spoke volumes before I stepped forward to do my part.

'I, Keith, take you, Stella, to be my wife,' I instructed clearly. As the rather puzzled looking young man repeated the words, Mary met my eye and gave me an encouraging wink. It was all going to be all right!

*   *   *

When I got back to the manse, Edmund called from the living room: 'Hey, your picture's in the paper, Cazza!'

'Oh no!' Feeling sick, I grabbed the *Echo* from him and tried to read as the two boys pressed around.

I managed to read the headline under my photograph, taken at the time of my ordination. 'Woman priest's blunder.'

It described my mistake, turning the pages over, and quoted from a diocesan statement that said the couple were legally married. It ended with a quote from Geoff giving me his full support and saying the couple, who had not been named, were being called back into

138

church to say their vows before witnesses.

From then on, the phone didn't stop ringing. Colleagues wanting to know how I was, and telling me their own horror stories of services that had gone wrong. Friends offering their sympathy and support. Members of the congregation including Gladys Eliot.

'That reporter woman was pokin' round at the Mothers' Union meetin' this afternoon,' she said. 'Askin' questions about yer—how we got on with yer—even wanted to know if you used bad language.'

'What did you say, Gladys?' I asked, holding my breath.

There was an answering intake of breath on the other end of the line. 'What d'yo think? Told her to bugger off, day I?' she said. 'Now, what I want to know is, how did they find out about this?'

Her shocked response when I told her about the anonymous letter was magnified on Sunday morning when Geoff used the theme of the trauma for his sermon.

'Most of you will have seen Carol's picture in the paper this week,' he said, 'in relation to a wedding she performed in this church. But what most of you won't know is that the newspaper found out about it, because someone, claiming to be a group from the congregation, sent an anonymous letter, to the *Echo*, and to the bishop!'

I was glad of the support of all the family,

including Sarah and Andy, in the pews. Standing in the stall in my chasuble and stole, I heard the gasp that reverberated round the pillars. I didn't dare look up, but I felt the loving glances, and those who looked the other way.

Geoff stood erect in the pulpit, a copy of the letter to the bishop in his hand. I had never seen the congregation so quiet, or him so angry.

'Anyway, to whoever sent this—and I can't believe, no matter what they claim, that it's anyone who worships here as part of our church family—I'd like to say that you have been unsuccessful. Myself, the church wardens and the whole diocese supports Carol's priestly ministry here, and will continue to do so! And *this* is what we think of your anonymous letters!'

CHAPTER TWENTY-TWO

There was another general gasp as the torn pieces of paper flew from Geoff's furious fingers out of the pulpit. They lay scattered like pieces of giant confetti in the crossing until Mary Watkins, coming up to assist at Communion, kicked them meaningfully to one side.

You could have heard a mouse cough as I began the Eucharistic prayer, hoping my voice wouldn't crack as I sang the familiar words: 'The Lord is here!'

'His Spirit is with us!' the congregation sang back, and I knew I did not imagine the new note of encouragement and loyalty that was in their tone.

As they came up to receive the sacrament, many squeezed my hand, and a few looked near to tears. If I had ever doubted my vocation to the priesthood, that Communion service put paid to those doubts forever.

There might be those who could not accept my ministry, who would clap their hands over this trauma my ineptitude had caused, and use it to prove their point that women should not exercise a priestly ministry. But the emotions of the congregation that day told me my enemies in Netherley Bank were very much in the minority. And my friends were sympathetic and sad I'd been hurt, and very angry, too!

'It wasn't us, Reverend Carol,' one little old lady quavered, her almost identical sister nodding at her side. 'We're very glad you're here!'

'Done marvellous for the kiddies, you have!'

'An' the old un's! We needed livenin' up!'

'I wish I could get my 'ands on the varmint who done it!'

'Thank you all so much!' I looked nonplussed from one to another of the familiar and new faces. I didn't know it then, but in the days that followed, I was going to get cards and flowers, jars of jam and boxes of chocolates, all from grateful and loving parishioners. The doorbell and telephone was going to be ceaselessly ringing as people came forward to express their support.

'I—I need to say the vestry prayer,' I said, quickly, escaping to the waiting choir.

As I finished the words of the dismissal, I could see that the choir, like the congregation, were shocked and dumbfounded by what Geoff had said.

'I hope he didn't think it's one of us!' elderly Gwen Simpson said grimly, breaking the silence.

'Yes. We were the only ones who really knew about it, Carol,' Stan, one of the basses, put in.

'It was all my fault!' I turned as Brenda Mountback looked across at me, tears streaming down her face. 'Oh Carol!' she sobbed, as I took her quietly into the corner. 'I feel terrible! I was the one who drew attention to the mistake! I'm sure nobody would've noticed otherwise!'

'Don't get upset, Brenda, there's no real harm been done,' I tried to reassure her. 'The best thing we can all do now is just forget any of it ever happened!'

'I—I can't!' Brenda confessed. 'Not after what you did for our Mom! Especially as we all know, really, who wrote the letters!'

At that precise moment, Clarke Pettisgrew swept in from the chancel where he had been talking to Geoff, his music in his hands and his face for once pale and thunderous. Clarke had not spoken a word in church, I realised, since the day Geoff announced he was leaving.

To my total amazement, Brenda went straight up to Clarke, through the ranks of the staring choir, and confronted him head on: 'Those anonymous letters to the bishop and the newspaper. You sent them, didn't you?'

There was a moment's stunned silence, as Clarke's pale face suffused with colour. Then he choked, his eyes almost bulging out of their sockets.

'Don't be ridiculous, woman!' he expostulated, and staring wildly from one to another of his pupils. 'You were all there in the choir that day! You heard the wedding fiasco!'

That word 'fiasco' was enough for me. As at

my side, I saw Mary, and behind her, Geoff, appearing in the doorway, I too turned to the spluttering Clarke.

'You did do it, didn't you, Clarke?' I challenged. 'Look, as Geoff's tried to point out this morning, there are proper channels to go through if you're not happy with anything that goes on here. The church wardens, the PCC.'

It was as if Clarke Pettisgrew finally exploded, the culmination of months of antagonism and seething hatred combining to turn his face into a mass of contorting purple emotions, all of them negative.

'I resign!' he almost screamed. 'The whole parish is unrecognisable and it's all your fault, you—you transvestite!'

As, still clad in his choir robes, he stormed out of the vestry door into the cool morning, never to be seen again, one of the basses said, meaningfully, 'Well, he's the only one still wearing a frock!'

CHAPTER TWENTY-THREE

'It all sounds very liberating and wonderful, darling,' said Mark, as we sat down to Sunday lunch, 'but what are you going to do without an organist?'

I shook my head, trying to sort my jumbled thoughts into order. 'Well, it's said Evensong tonight, and we don't have music at the mid-week services.'

'So you've got until next Sunday to replace the maestro?' Mark dropped a kiss on my head. 'Better start praying, darling!'

At Evensong, we prayed for unity within our parish, especially when Geoff had gone. To my surprise I noticed a few faces who normally just attended the morning service, and a couple who didn't come to church at all!

'Dawn and Wayne! It's great to see you here!' I exclaimed, as the Masons came rather self-consciously to shake hands after the service. 'Sorry I haven't been able to get round to see you since the hospital service, but I've been pretty busy.'

Wayne grinned. 'We know, we've seen your picture in the paper,' he said. 'That's one reason we wanted to come tonight—to tell you we're on your side, and the other, well . . .'

He looked at Dawn who I noticed for the first time, was looking particularly radiant. 'I'm pregnant, Reverend Carol!' she told me, excitedly. 'We were hoping before we saw you at the hospital, but now I've been to the doctors, and it's definite!'

'Oh Dawn, that's marvellous news!' After all they had been through, I felt so happy for them I could've danced! 'This baby is the answer to all the prayers we've been saying for you these past few months. Not to replace Simon, you could never do that. But for his or her own sake!'

'We know, Reverend Carol,' the young woman replied, 'that's why you've got to do the christening—an extra special one!'

Her husband grinned and gave me a mischievous nudge before they left the church. 'Just so long as you remember to say all the words!' he said, meaningfully.

Another unexpected worshipper that evening was Bob Grainger. I was glad to see him because an idea had been nudging at me since my lunchtime conversation with Mark.

'Bob?' I began as we walked automatically towards the garden of remembrance. 'Didn't you once tell me you used to play the organ in church?'

The widower nodded. 'Well, yes, I was very keen as a lad at the old Holy Trinity,' he said, 'but I haven't played for a long time. Why do you ask, Reverend Carol?'

I took a deep breath, and instinctively knowing I could trust him, told him about the

146

scene in the vestry after the morning Eucharist.

'The director of music has walked out,' I finished worriedly, 'and until we can advertise and fill the gap, we're pretty desperate.'

Bob gave one of his rare smiles. 'You must be, if you've asked me,' he said. 'Tell you what, I'll check the boys are all right, and then we'll go back into the church if you've got time and I'll see how much I can remember.'

By the time I got back to the manse I was able to tell Mark that my prayers for a new organist had at least been temporarily answered.

'Bob's going to come over and practise as much as he can in the week,' I said, as I picked up the telephone to let Geoff know what I'd done. 'One good thing is that Clarke never played anything modern, so he won't have to learn anything new!'

My spirits lifted, I told Mark the other piece of good news of the evening, about Dawn and Wayne's new baby. 'So thank God, from starting as a pretty fraught day, it's ending up pretty marvellous!' I said with relief.

Pulling off my dog collar, I went into the living room, where the boys were having one of their impromptu wrestling matches on the hearth.

In a thoroughly silly mood now, I sat on top of the tangled arms and legs and the yells and chortles of laughter rose to a crescendo, accompanied as usual by Gran's snores, Becky's frenzied barking and Jacob's dash upstairs.

'What's all the noise?' called Mark, coming down the hall. 'If you two don't . . . !'

'It's Cazza!' Edmund protested, in mock indignation, his partly shaved head bobbing up alongside his brother's tousled mop.

'Yes!' Berkley piped up, as I sprang away, pretending innocence. 'She starts it, then we get told off!'

'Behave yourself, you!' Mark came in, wagging his finger at me, and pulled me into his arms.

'No snoggin' allowed!' Berkley said automatically, as he picked up the TV remote control.

As, still hand in hand, we sat down on the sofa, it was suddenly good just to be home.

CHAPTER TWENTY-FOUR

My complacency lasted until the next morning when, after our prayers, Geoff informed me that Clarke Pettisgrew had been to see him on Sunday afternoon.

'He's handed in his official resignation, which is what we expected,' he said, as he led the way towards the vicarage, 'but what I didn't really anticipate happening quite so fast is he's announced he intends taking most of the early morning congregation and some of the eleven o'clockers with him!'

I sighed, realising all Geoff's earlier fears were to be realised. If Clarke had his way, our church family would be split and diminished. 'No use asking where they're going, of course,' I said, as Geoff nodded grimly. 'Father Brian and his flying bishop will be really clapping their hands!'

'It's not all one-sided though, Carol,' Geoff said, as he neatly side-stepped one of the empty packing cases which had suddenly begun to appear in the vicarage. 'I was talking to Brian's church warden the other day and he says some of the congregation are really upset by his attitude towards women priests. Apparently, he's taken to getting up in the pulpit talking about hell fire and priestesses, and it's not going down too well with some people.'

'So maybe we'll be doing a swap. We'll be getting some of his while he gets Clarke's lot!' I said, thoughtfully. 'I'm sure God's got it all worked out in the end!'

'I expect you're right,' said my colleague, as we went into the kitchen. 'Incidentally, the other piece of news I've got is that Bishop Paul wants to see you as soon as possible.'

Instinctively feeling like a naughty schoolgirl, I stared at him. 'Oh no, what's he going to do?'

Geoff smiled. 'Keep calm,' he said. 'He just wants you to ring and make an appointment for a chat. I'm sure you've got nothing to worry about!'

A chat with the bishop, undoubtedly about my faux pas with the wedding, could not be good news. I rang his secretary as soon as I got back to my study and was told he could see me in a week's time.

A whole week of wondering what was going to happen, whether Bishop Paul would exercise his right to discipline or even dismiss me for my negligence. Bishops were, I knew, a law unto themselves.

I was hardly in the mood for Gwyneth Armstrong, banging grimly on the front door with her reporter's notebook in her hand. 'I wasn't in church yesterday,' she said, following me doggedly inside. 'What's all this about anonymous letters being torn up?'

Resignedly, I told her the facts. 'I don't think we need put anything in the magazine, Gwyneth,' I finished, as she frowned thoughtfully at me through her specs. 'It's all over bar the shouting, and the bishop'll probably do that when I go to see him next Thursday.'

Persuading her to go and visit Geoff to get his final editorial, I went back to my study, and there in the silence, lit a candle.

'Please, Lord,' I prayed, thinking of my conversation with Geoff, 'help us through these traumas and changes. Give us such an awareness of your peace inside us that as we lose people and hopefully gain new ones, we remain always in your love.'

There was so much to pray for: for Bob, as he practised for Sunday, for Geoff as he prepared to leave us, for the church and its wardens, approaching the interregnum, for myself as I awaited my interview with Bishop Paul.

In those quiet moments, set apart from the busy world outside, I knew there was no better place I could be, and no more important thing I could be doing than saying my prayers.

As often happens, it wasn't only those particular prayers which got answered during the course of the next week. Bob Grainger, though nervous and self-effacing, played Sunday's four hymns as well as he knew how. More important, at the beginning of the service, when I introduced him to the congregation and described how he had agreed to step into the breach of Clarke's unfortunate indisposition, he was warmly applauded.

'So long as they don't mind having the same hymns more than once, Reverend Carol,' he said, as I congratulated him in the vestry. 'That was nearly all my repertoire! And so long as the singers know I'm no choir master!'

'Don't worry, love!' Smiling, Brenda Mountback put a motherly arm around him. 'We lot 've bin directed so much over the years we can run on automatic pilot, can't we, kids?'

'It might be nice to come along to choir practice though—er—Bob,' Geoff suggested, diplomatically. 'Then they can tell you what they sing!'

The whole atmosphere at church seemed much more joyful and relaxed, and, as if in direct answer to my prayer, united, too. As if, with the discontented ones elsewhere, we really could be one big happy family at last.

I was still rejoicing when I got the sudden telephone call from Stella Tonks. 'Can you pop round and see us, Reverend Carol?' she asked, sounding worryingly anxious. 'As soon as possible?'

'I'll come straight away, Stella,' I said. Putting the phone down, I turned to Mark. 'Stella wants to see me. I hope it's nothing to do with the wedding. If—if the newspapers have tracked them down it could be really embarrassing for them even now.'

'I'll take you round,' Mark offered. 'Come on, darling. Don't look so worried.'

When we reached the flat, he sat in the car while I went up to the door. I was praying as I walked. Stella and Keith had been so good about my mistake but there was a limit to what anyone could stand.

Stella's nervous look as she opened the door did nothing to allay my fears. 'Keith's taken Antonia to his mom's, so I thought it would be a good time for us to talk,' she said, leading me into the comfortable living room.

'There's something I wanted to ask you, but I was too embarrassed, those times we came to church. It's about christening.'

I frowned in surprise. 'But I thought Antonia had been christened,' I said. 'Didn't you say something about doing things the wrong way round?'

Stella sighed, her blue eyes suddenly troubled. 'Not Antonia, Reverend Carol, me!' she explained. 'For some reason, my mom and dad never had me done, and when we booked the wedding, the other vicar said it didn't matter so long as one of us had been, and Keith has so that was okay.'

'But?' I waited, and the young woman took a deep breath and then began: 'I prob'ly wouldn't have bothered if you hadn't made the mistake in the wedding and made us go back

153

to church. But well, going back saying the words in the quiet, it was all so special. It was like God wanted us there for a reason, and I haven't been able to stop thinking about him since.'

'So you want to learn more about him—to get baptised?' I asked, scarcely able to breathe for the joy and wonder of it all. I explained that in the case of adults, confirmation usually followed baptism. 'But I'm sure we can arrange some special classes, if you're really interested.'

Stella's eyes met mine, full of relief and excitement. 'It's like he's interested in me, Reverend Carol,' she explained, shyly. 'Does that make sense to you?'

As a noise at the front door heralded the return of Keith and Antonia, I nodded, so elated I felt I could've flown.

To a convert like myself, it made all the sense in the world!

CHAPTER TWENTY-FIVE

'I've had another letter about you!' Bishop Paul said bluntly, as he closed the door of his study, and then, seeing the look on my face, 'It's all right, my dear, this one's not anonymous, far from it.'

Wonderingly, I took the bundle of papers he handed me. My heart skipped a beat as I recognised the flowing handwriting and lucid style of Gwyneth Armstrong:

'We, the undersigned, wish to pledge our support of our wonderful woman priest, Reverend Carol Hathorne,' it began. 'She is undoubtedly the best and most caring minister we have had in this parish for many years.'

Hurriedly turning from the rest of Gwyneth's paragraphs of purple praise, I turned the page. Tears filled my eyes as I saw signature after signature, from Marcie Danks and Des, who had made a 'D' on the page, to the carefully inscribed signature of the proprietor of Willow Tree nursing home. Even the Encounter children had signed their names.

'She must have gone all over the parish,' I exclaimed, as I handed the bundle back to the bishop. 'Heaven knows what gossip she'll have picked up for next month's magazine!'

'Well,' said the bishop, discreetly pushing a

box of tissues in my direction, 'this just confirms what I knew already—that the people at St Benedict's really love you and the business about the anonymous letters and the wedding were just a lot of eyewash. That's really all I wanted to say to you, Carol.'

Feeling more able to relax now, I told him about my conversation with Stella. 'If she comes to classes she could perhaps be baptised on Easter Eve next year,' I planned. 'Then confirmed shortly afterwards with our other young candidates.'

'It's certainly a resurrection story,' Bishop Paul said, almost to himself. 'I'll be very interested to hear how Stella progresses. And I'll also be interested in what you get up to, in this pending interregnum!'

'I reckon they'll probably forget about advertising for a new incumbent,' Mark said, as we took our walk in the coppice that afternoon. 'As far as the congregation is concerned, you're the vicar, the one they send for when they want to talk about God.'

'Is that a Methodist definition?' I grinned. 'If so, you're a vicar, too, a flying one with your congregations!'

He took advantage of Gran pausing to eat some grass, to kiss me under the tree where, last year, we had some of our wedding photographs taken.

'Not me, I'm an albeit!' he said. 'As I read about someone somewhere "a man of the cloth—albeit a Methodist!"'

'Labels again,' I reproved playfully, as we continued on our way. 'There's only one label I want to wear. It says "God loves me" and "I love you".'

'That's two labels,' my husband replied, and it reminds me of a song. 'God loves you and I love you, and that's the way it should be!'

We sang the song as we made our way back onto the path that led to the church. Above it, the vicarage was already beginning to look empty, curtains down and the garage packed with boxes.

It was Geoff's final Sunday that week and a fine party was given for him and his family in the parish centre, with gifts presented and speeches made by the church wardens and other VIP's.

'It's going to be really strange without you,' I said. 'Nobody to call on in times of crisis, like ferrets and missing wedding vows. And heaven knows what we'll do without you, young Katie, at Merrily Mall next Sunday!'

Katie grinned, looking very much like her dad in that moment. 'Michelle's going to do my part in the play, aren't you?' she asked the blonde-haired figure I'd only just noticed at her side. 'I told her we were desperate!'

'We are, Michelle. Thank you for—um—volunteering,' I said gratefully.

As the two girls went off, arm in arm, Geoff laughed. 'I can see I'd better watch it,' he said.

157

'I've obviously got another embryonic organising woman priest there!'

The following Saturday, we stood by the manse wall and waved the removal van out of sight down the High Street.

'That's it, then, darling!' Mark said, as we turned and went back indoors. 'St Benedict's interregnum starts here!'

In Evening Prayer that night, we prayed for Geoff and his family as they began a new chapter in their ministry and we also prayed for Netherley Bank, both parish and circuit, that we would be guided and supported during the next few months.

At two thirty the next afternoon, a hopeful, nervous group of us trooped into the central arena at Merrily Mall. Driving here had been a nightmare, with so many queues of traffic, all heading for this Mecca of a shopping city. Parking had been difficult, and we had had to split up, even with the limited number of vehicles we had brought with us.

But thankfully, Rev Derrick Jones was here to direct us in the technicalities like microphones and speakers.

'Welcome to our service,' Mark announced from the raised dais. 'And this week, our worship is led by the youngsters of St Benedict's church, Netherley Bank.'

'Oooh, miss—I'm scared!'

'Oh no, me auntie's over theer!'

'Miss! Miss!'

'Yes, Michelle?' I looked down patiently at the golden-haired youngster at my side.

She gulped. 'I dow think I c'n do it, miss! Read all these words!'

I squeezed her shoulder encouragingly, though inwardly I was dismayed. 'Course you can, Michelle!' I said. 'I feel like that every Sunday morning, just before I stand up in church. After the first sentence, you'll be fine!'

Michelle looked from me to the swirling crowds. 'I dunno, miss,' she muttered. 'I'd still rather go shoppin'!'

Next moment, she was on the podium and beginning the words of the script: 'Once upon a time, there were two brothers. They were always stealing.'

As we had hoped, people stopped to watch and listen. Later, when the play finished and hymn singing began, led by a member of Mark's congregation, many of them drifted away.

But it didn't matter, because who knew what would come from the seeds that were being sown today?

The church in the market place, I thought, with its roots in that enormous building on Barlow Hill. And roots that went back even further, to the cross itself.

We had just congratulated our participants and were preparing to leave the shopping centre when a familiar quavering voice called from behind us, 'Here, darlin', wait for us!'

Turning, I saw Daisy Jenkins, and Tom, walking for the first time since his illness.

'They tode we yo was comin' ere vicar,' Tom said, as they caught up with us. 'My Uncle Zechaniah, yer know, 'e was one of the fust who worked the furnaces in these parts, and he once sed ter me . . .'

'Never mind that now, Tommy.' Stopping at a bench near one of the ornamental fountains, Daisy delved into the enormous purple and green carpet bag she was carrying.

'A little summat I run up for yo' an' yer hubby, darlin',' she beamed, pressing a squashy carrier bag into my hands. 'Just a little token.'

We sat on the bench to open it, Tom and Daisy standing expectantly at our side.

'Oh.' There didn't seem anything else to say for a moment. I was speechless as I lifted out what was inside. 'Er look, Mark, matching yellow shirts.'

'With—um—red polka dots,' he swallowed. 'They—they'll be very nice, for our day off.'

Daisy tutted and shook her pink rinsed head. 'Day off nuthin',' she declared. 'Dow yer see, I've put a little space round the necks? That's specially for yer dog collars to fit in, ay it?'

POSTSCRIPT

It was Easter Eve at St Benedict's, Netherley Bank, and I didn't need to look in the service register to see we had more than doubled last year's attendance figures.

The great church had been in complete darkness and people shivered as much with anticipation as with the cold as I blessed and lit the Easter candle inserting incense into it at the bonfire outside the porch.

'The light of Christ!' I sang the ancient acclamation, traditionally the deacon's job, as I led the procession, all holding small candles. They followed, the Methodists, youngsters, and non-churchgoers all mingled with regulars. Those who were familiar with it made the response:

'Thanks be to God!'

As the Gospel was read by Mark, the candles were lit, and the bells rung. The Gloria was sung by our choir, heralding the start of the church's new year after the bleakness of Good Friday. Brenda Mountback's voice, deep and golden, swelled, and she met my eyes in a moment of trust and mutual understanding that was hard to put into words.

A few lights were switched on at a given signal and then the great building seemed to glow, so full it was with shimmering glory. The light was shining right through to the heart of me, in pride and gratitude as the baptism party went to the font.

The congregation turned and watched as Stella made her baptism promises, the promises she would soon be reiterating when she was confirmed next week with the children from Encounter. In recent months, it had been so good to see her faith emerging as she studied and prayed and worked, and I knew how privileged I was to be able to teach her and also to learn from her. She had become known and loved by many in our church, though only Mary and Sally knew the full story of how she came to be there.

'Stella Louise, I baptise you.' The ritual was, as the bishop had said, all about resurrection. It was all about renewal, too. I thought of the early church, and the promises that were made and it all made sense, what we were doing, and also what we failed to do. I was dizzy with wonder that sometimes, as in Stella's case, and against all the odds, we succeeded, and the Gospel got through, in spite of, as much as because of, our efforts.

I turned, my heart beating fast as Stella got down, and someone else moved to my side, silently handing me a tiny, white wrapped bundle of new life. 'Name this child,' I asked.

For a moment, Dawn and Wayne Mason's young-again faces swam in front of me. Then, swallowing my tears, I declared joyfully:

'Simone Anne, I baptize you in the name of the Father, the Son, and the Holy Spirit. Amen.'